Homesteader's Daughter
99 years on Dakota Prairie

Life and times of

Joyce Dole-Anderson

Authored by

Gary W. Wietgrefe

Transcripts from 1984 Beld family history
by

Grace Albertha Beld-Vander Veen

Produced by GWW Books
Rapid City, SD

 Though not copyrighted, the Beld family history of 1984 by Grace Albertha Beld-Vander Veen was made available for this publication with use permission by Joyce Dole-Anderson.

GWW Books, 1811 Sunny Springs Dr., Rapid City, SD 57702.
Website: www.RelatingtoAncients.com
Email: gwwbooks@outlook.com
Quantity orders: special discounts are available on quantity purchases by schools, book clubs, organizations, businesses, and others. Submit a request at www.RelatingtoAncients.com, or gwwbooks@outlook.com.
Print credits: Book production: GWW Books, Rapid City, SD.
Photos: Grace Albertha Beld-Vander Veen collection
Cover design by Gary W. Wietgrefe
Font: Garamond
Name: Wietgrefe, Gary W, 1953---, author.
Title: Homesteader's Daughter
Subtitle: 99 years on Dakota Prairie

Identifiers: Paperback ISBN 9798994196830

Subjects: Nonfiction: History
Classification: 1. HIS036090 History/United States/State & Local/Midwest/SD;
2. REL012000 Religion/Christian Living/General;
3. BIO022000 Biography & Autobiography/woman;

First Edition. First Printing. Printed in United States of America.

Dedicated to my friend and neighbor, Joyce Anderson, and all children and grandchildren of homesteaders.

Author's Note

Most homesteaders were literate. Education, especially reading, limited by constant work, was provided by Christian churches, itinerant (usually male) teachers, and one-room public schools where oldest daughters of settlers taught. As the oldest daughter of (1911) German-Russian immigrants, my mother, ten years older than her next sibling, taught in her very rural South Dakota one-room school following her mother's career as a teacher and farmwife.

As you will read, this John Beld homesteading story starts with his explanation written if excellent English. Born in 1870, John explained where his family came from (Germany and Holland to Michigan), why they moved to western South Dakota, and what they had to do to survive. As testament to continual education, John's youngest daughter, Grace, the eighth child, born on the Dakota prairie, was obligated to pick up the family story from her birth into a family dialogue printed in 1984.

My contribution, as a second generation American and lifelong South Dakotan, is to provide twenty-first century readers the context of forgotten terms, pioneering techniques, and technology adopted by homesteaders.

The original book sequence, paragraphs, and wording has only been modified when necessary to aid the story's flow. May my supplemental commentary provide more understanding of early Dakota development.

Contents

Introduction

This is a true story.

The last Dakota homesteaders had it worse than others. As the last American pioneers, on what little farmable ground remained, water was key. Pre-history onward settlements were near water and crops grown to sustain a family and trade—except the last homesteaders. They took what ground was left in the dryest part of South Dakota farthest from water.

How did women cook, clean, bath, and do laundry? Cattle were fenced by water. Women hauled it.

Before rain barrels were installed below eves until cisterns were dug, water was brought to the sod house by buckets, rationed, and valued. First, it had to rain. Before wells, creeks ran dry.

A mattress was not brought to save limited space in their emigrant boxcar. Grass was too short for bedding.

As the modest homesteader's daughter explained, "Water…was a mile and a half away so it made them really meek. The weather was hot and dry, not much grass upon the (unfenced) land because ranchers had cattle and sheep that ate it to the sand. Before the time of getting coal, they would burn cow chips for heat."

Then it got tough…. Resourcefulness was key.

Historical Background

After the Civil War (1861-1865) immigrants from eastern states, primarily from Europe, homesteaded most of South Dakota. They came for different reasons. Opportunity to own enough land for an economically viable farm was important but not the exclusive reason. Some came to seek a healthier climate.

Even in the early twentieth century, immunizations were not available for many diseases like tuberculosis, smallpox, and others. Seeking health drove settlers west. Tuberculosis encouraged the Beld family to move from Michigan to western South Dakota. Though the disease took many lives, the family multiplied and spread.

Those healthy and unwilling or lacked skills to farm, went west for opportunity. Gold seeking in the Mountains encouraged thousands. Populating the Plains, those with retail and trade skills found ample opportunities post-Civil War through the 1920s at new railheads towns.

Work was available for anyone--ambitious or not. As Helen Cody Wetmore (Buffalo Bill's younger sister) wrote in 1899, "*In frontier days a man had but to ask for work to get it. There was enough and to spare for every one.*"[1]

Work equaled survival for the Beld family.

---

[1]Helen Cody Wetmore, Buffalo Bill—Last of the Great Scouts, The Life Story of Colonel William F. Cody, A Bison Book, University of Nebraska Press, 1965 (reproduced from the 1899 edition), p. 149.

Character Profile
Joyce Dole-Anderson

Family	Name	Born/Died[2]
Self	Joyce Dole-Anderson	July 5, 1926
Husband	George E. Anderson	Sep. 13, 1920 Dec. 25, 2008
Father	Martin Dole	Dec. 23, 1895 Dec. 8, 1962
Mother	Getrude "Gertie" Beld-Dole	June 3, 1895 Jan. 23, 1981
Maternal grandfather	John Beld Married Gertie in 1889	July 25, 1870 Aug. 20, 1961
Maternal grandmother	Gurtrude "Gertie" Heetderks-Beld	Aug. 24, 1868 April 19, 1944
Maternal great grandfather	Henry John Beld	Oct. 23, 1840 Nov. 8, 1895
Maternal great grandmother	Anje Belo-Bos-Beld-Blerum	Feb. 26. 1847 July 28, 1893
Brother	Severn Maurice Dole	Jan. 7, 1924
Brother	Henry John Dole	Oct. 16, 1928
Sister	Anna Jean Dole-Vande Kieft	Feb. 12, 1933, June 18, 2024
Brother	Marvin Gerard Dole	June 13, 1937
Sister	Lorraine Anderson	Sep. 23, 1938 April 14, 2014
Adopted son	Dean Lee Anderson	Aug. 26, 1941
Adopted daughter	Linda Rae Anderson	Nov. 12, 1943
Adopted daughter	Joan Marie Anderson	Sep. 3, 1946
Adopted daughter	Betty Lou Anderson	Jan. 10, 1949
Adopted twin daughter	Judy Mae Anderson	July 27, 1955
Adopted twin daughter	Jolene Kay Anderson	July 27, 1955
Son	Bradley Wayne Anderson	Aug. 22, 1963
Adopted son	Bruce Eugene Anderson	Mar. 21, 1968

[2] Some birth and death dates conflict in Beld family records.

Chapter 1
Homesteading

Homesteaders that settled the U.S. are gone. Stories of their arrival are rare. Specifically, why did they come to South Dakota?

Where did they originate? Many came from other countries, mostly Europe. Why did they leave Europe. Where did they settle upon arrival?

Nearly all South Dakota homesteaders came from states that no longer offered the homestead option.

Was it just free land and an opportunity to own 160 acres?

Most did not have money to purchase land. How did they make a living before the first crops were harvested?

It took a minimum of six months to plow, level, till, plant and harvest the first crop. What did they eat?

Where did they get food and other supplies?

How far did they have to travel to get building materials, farm supplies, and food?

How did they get to a town to pick up supplies?

Some arrived with families. What did the children do? Did they have toys to play with? Where did they go to school?

Who can answer those questions about South Dakota homesteaders?

Dakota Territory was established in 1861, though Homesteading in South Dakota started in 1863. The Beld family were some of the last South Dakota homesteaders. Why wasn't that government land claimed earlier? Was it too dry, too rocky, or to remote to draw settlers?

If too dry and too remote, where did they get water for cattle and home use?

What was their shelter before a home was built?

What kind of home did they build?

How long did it take them to build their first home?

Was their first shelter temporary? If so, how long did they live in it before building a better home?

Did they have windows, doors, a roof, cook stove and some type of heater to keep warm? What was their fuel?

Most came with clothes on their backs and little more. How did they build their first home? Did they have help?

Weren't they isolated?

Those that were U.S. residents and agreed to homestead had to make certain land improvements, including raising crops for at least five years, and have a residence on the land at least six months each year to meet homestead requirements.

The Homestead Act of 1862 allocated 160 acres within a plotted township of thirty-six sections (square miles) of 640 acres. That means there were a minimum of four residences in each section—meaning neighbors were no more than a half mile away. Right?

Could they make a living on land earlier settlers rejected?

With so many neighbors did they have social gatherings and help each other?

Above are a few questions answered in this exciting chapter of American and South Dakota history.

Ninety-nine-year-old Joyce Anderson who currently lives in Rapid City as a widow, shares her family story on how they came to American, when they came, why they came, and why they eventually moved to a South Dakota and homesteaded. Their sweat, trials, and opportunities are the definition of tenacity.

Chapter 2

Lost

Have you ever been lost?

Lost has many meanings. It would be common to think about being a child and lost in a large department store. At two foot tall—it's a jungle of rows, shelves, clothes in racks or tables under which to hide.

I've been geographically lost. Not to the extent of heart throbbing, but lost on the water.

The Oahe Dam, closed the natural flow of the Missouri River in 1962, was dedicated as the world's largest earthen dam by President John F. Kennedy August 17, 1962. My wife was there with her family—disappointed in losing their ground, but excited to see the youngest president (about a year before he was assassinated).

My in-laws lived, farmed, and ranched north of Oahe Dam and were the first family forced from their ground due to readily available gravel needed for road construction.

Oahe Dam, a few miles north of the state capitol, was blocked by a massive dirt pile about two-hundred and fifty feet deep and a mile across backing up water two hundred miles north.

Each creek, gully, and river draining into Oahe created wind-protected fishing spots along the rocky shores. I got lost in more than one of those inlets.

One day on a calm morning in the 1980s a friend and I launched early from Cow Creek, headed out into the calm Oahe expanses before a heavy fog set in. We were already trolling the shoreline for walleyes when the fog got so thick we couldn't see the shore. It was hard to tell, maybe we could see only ten feet from our boat…lost.

We kept the motor running and boat trolling slowly to keep fishing while our Lowrance depth finder whirled radar signals of water depth.

Lost. Yes, but we didn't panic.

Always on heightened alert to avoid a muddy island or rocky point, we were anxious.

Key to surviving being lost is to not panic, but use your God-given senses—sight, sound, and brain to analyze the situation.

You may ask, why didn't you use your Lowrance depth finder and its built-in maps of Missouri's underwater terrain?

I had what I thought was one of the best depth finders on the market. It displayed a circular radar screen (similar to those in airplanes) with a rotating beacon marking the depth, and occasionally fish.

Technology tends to drive us from God-given senses to reliance on gadgets.

Though Darrell Lowrance introduced fishing depth finders in 1957, global positioning (GPS) maps were not available until the late 1980s into the 1990s. Now sports fishermen just coordinate their depth-finder with trolling motor to remain on a desirable path.

Back to being lost.

Dawn had sprung but the fog obliqued the sun. So it was not possible to see the eastern sun while we trolled.

Water provides amazing acoustics. We could hear fishermen's boat motors in the distance—a mile or two. Who knows? None appeared in the fog.

I am convinced Jesus preached to a crowd on shore using water's acoustics by having fisherman, Peter, push off from shore.[3]

Now, when people are asked what they would do if lost, they likely would say, "I'd use my cell phone to call for help, or use the mapping app to extricate myself." Cell phones are just another common excuse not to use natural senses.

---

[3] Luke 5:1-11 A large crowd had gathered around Jesus to hear what he was preaching. Jesus asked Simon Peter to use his boat that he might push off from shore. Jesus sat and preached.

Having grown up on South Dakota's prairie, I knew fog occurs when high humidity and temperature form a dew point and not dispensed by wind. As the sun rises, it heats the air igniting prairie winds which drives down humidity dispersing the fog.

Lost and found. After the morning fog dissolved, we realized we were several bays from where we thought we were.

Later in the day when back on shore, fish stories were not how a big one got away, but how fog unsettled fishermen.

I start this book with a lost story, because as you will read the Beld family settled twenty-one miles of open prairie from the nearest town. No roads. One grass-covered rise looked like the nest.

Later, while walking for necessities in the dead of winter seven miles to the nearest store, the mother wouldn't let the young girls rest. Fear the cold would freeze them in place, or possibly white-out blowing snow would confuse their directions. Don't get lost if you can prevent it.

Belds lost their home country do to government religious restrictions.

Belds lost family from disease and lost many children by premature death.

One brother accompanied his brother from their South Dakota sod house to Michigan because a wife was lost from childbirth.

Belds kept their faith in God, established churches, raised families and found their way homesteading on barren prairie.

Chapter 3

Joyce Dole-Anderson Memories

This author's notes comprise this chapter from various discussions with Joyce. At ninety-nine, she has a fantastic memory. Any errors in this dialogue are strictly my poor memory and note-taking.

"My dad was picked up by this couple in Grand Rapids, Michigan when he was five and gave him a note 'Martin Dole'. De Jong might have been his original name. He ended up ten miles southeast of Lodgepole," South Dakota.

Where did you go to school?

"Hubbard School—a mile north of our place. The first years I went there were grades one, two, three, and four. I went there and later taught at Hubbard School after getting my teaching certificate at Northern State Teachers College in Aberdeen.

"After high school 1944-1945 then again 1945-1946 I taught. Got married June 28, 1946.

"George lived on his family's home place. He took care of his invalid mother who died in 1943. Then he took care of his father. Took him to Bismarck (ND) in 1945 and died of heart trouble.

"George was born in that house where they lived. And we lived there until moving here (on Sunny Springs Dr., Rapid City, SD) in 2005."

"He is buried in Duck Creek Lutheran Church Cemetery. The church was built in 1933. That is where we went to Church.

"We both taught Sunday School there. George was a good singer. Liked to sing.

"We adopted three girls in 1953 and adopted Dean in 1955. The twins in 1959. They were three and half years old. Our son Brad was born in 1963. Then we adopted Bruce in 1968.

"Brad is a doctor, and executive director here at Monument Health. He graduated from Oral Roberts University.

"Son, Bruce, graduated from Concordia in St. Paul."

Testament to Joyce's mothering instincts she put extra effort into adopting children. Life was tough. Funds were limited for George and Joyce. Rather than using time nurturing dogs or cats, common today, she raised children.

Joyce went on, "We adopted seven children. Three girls had an older brother. At first, I was not aware of him. I was twenty-seven and Linda was ten.

"Abbott House in Mitchell took Dean in 1955. I was only fifteen years older than him. Parents were alcoholics.

"My mother said she was born in Grant, Newaygo County, Michigan. When they decided to move and homestead in South Dakota, they took a boat to Chicago where the family boarded a train to Hettinger, North Dakota. That was the closest place on the rail.

"Their belongings were in a boxcar with three other families. They had to stay in Hettinger a few days until the La Febres came with their wagon.

"Grandpa Beld was born in Beaverdam, Ottawa County, Michigan. He met Gertie Heetderks in 1889 and got married in 1891.

"I was sixteen when George and I became interested in each other. He was six years older than me. We'd now be married seventy-nine years.

"I wanted to be a June bride, he was always so busy haying in June.

"We waited four years to get married because he was busy taking care of his parents and farming.

"George was a worker and a thinker.

"He had a wind charger with a generator hooked to batteries in the basement. That gave lights to our house.

"George dug a six-foot deep trench from the windmill to the house by hand. Then dug a cistern.

"When the girls were adopted, we got electricity."

When did you get rural electricity?

"REA[4] came in 1953. We knew a church missionary and gave him our wind generator. He took it to Africa.

"Our water wasn't good. We hauled water from Lodgepole for washing clothes because our water was so hard.

"After we got electricity, we got a water softener so we could wash clothes with our well water."

How deep was your well?

"I'm not sure—shallow enough to pump it with a windmill into the cistern by the house. The electricity would pump it into the house.

"George was always thinking. He went seven years to school. He skipped a grade, so he had an eighth grade education."

I understand your mother was a young girl when

---

[4] REA is United States Department of Agriculture's Rural Electric Administration.

your grandparents homesteaded in Perkins County (SD) in 1908. Tell me about that.

"Grandpa and his brother and other families came together with their stuff in a boxcar. They didn't have much and not much room. Rather than bringing mattresses, they figured they would just stuff grass in bedding. Well, when they got to their homestead ground in July, there was no grass to clip. Cattle and sheep had grazed it off.

"They slept on the ground. It took my grandfather nine days to build their sod house. Families helped each other.

"They couldn't afford much. Only a few boards for the roof. The first Sunday they had church services and it started to rain afterwards. Grandpa and grandma got under an umbrella and the kids hunched together under the table.

"Grandpa worked for Le Febre then found work in Lemmon so they could buy a door and floor boards for their sod house. He dug a basement for a bar and one for Mr. Smith. Smith then wanted a fence. He also had an electric machine. Grandpa worked on steam engines but not electricity. But, he did it and earned enough money to close their house for winter."

Where did your grandma get groceries?

(Joyce didn't give the year, but told this story.)

"Mom (Gerdie) told me they had to walk seven miles to Lodgepole and home with supplies. Mom begged grandma to buy an orange so they could suck on it on the way home. It was very hot.

"In wintertime when they walked home from Lodgepole it was so cold carrying groceries. Mother wanted to lay down and rest, but grandmother wouldn't let her. She said, 'Because we would never get up.'

"One time, a storm was too bad. They walked as far as Parker's and Henry Van Duines. They had a horse. Grandma and mother walked home beside the horse to protect from the storm.

When wagons were too full, kids walked.

In the spring of 1912 Joyce's mother, Gerdie, walked to their homestead over thirty miles in one day from Lemmon to seven miles southwest of Lodgepole.

"To get water, my mother, Gerdie, had to walk a mile to the pond. Then had to boil it.

"Jennie and Annie, my mother's oldest sisters, worked in a hotel in Lemmon. My mother worked there, too. She was able to save $33.00 that year. Her father, my grandfather John Beld, needed her $33.00 to pay taxes.

"Mom worked hard and saved, but she finally gave it to him. But, they eventually lost the place later when Uncle Will was on it.

"(In the 1930s) my father didn't lose his farm. He got feed loans and sent his cows to Martin, South Dakota. They kept two cows, and two horses. They didn't have a car.

"Saturdays, the manure spreader was used for barn-cleaning. Then it was cleaned. We rode in the manure wagon to church—Holland Center Church on Sunday.

"Bad, bad dust storms. Too bad couldn't go anyplace.

"Then the grasshoppers came. Don't forget the grasshoppers!

"Mom and I washed clothes on the board until we got a wash machine in 1937. I was born in 1926.

"Sam Dole had a threshing machine. He was not honest and nobody would work for him. So, (my husband) George's dad ran the thresh machine and people worked for him in Briceland, Minnesota.

"We were poorest of the poor. We didn't have a horse, so we walked to school. (Husband) George had a horse. My brother Henry trained a steer as a horse and rode it like a horse. Then, finally, rode it to the truck when dad sold it in the fall.

"We never got to play. All we knew was work. We didn't have toys. Well, Severn got a little truck from a school teacher.

"First we lived in Aberdeen and went to Bison. My father paved the roads (as in using a type of road grader to occasionally smooth out the roads). Perkins County went broke. Dad never got paid. He still had to pay the lady in Bison where we stayed.

"When we lived in Bison, mom found a little doll without a head and gave it to me, but I wouldn't play with it.

"My folks were poorest of poor.

"Dad put two houses together. Shacks. Didn't know where he got the wood from. They were about twelve foot wide and longer. I don't know how long they were. The second shack was about the same size and Dad put it at ninety degree angle which double the size of our house."

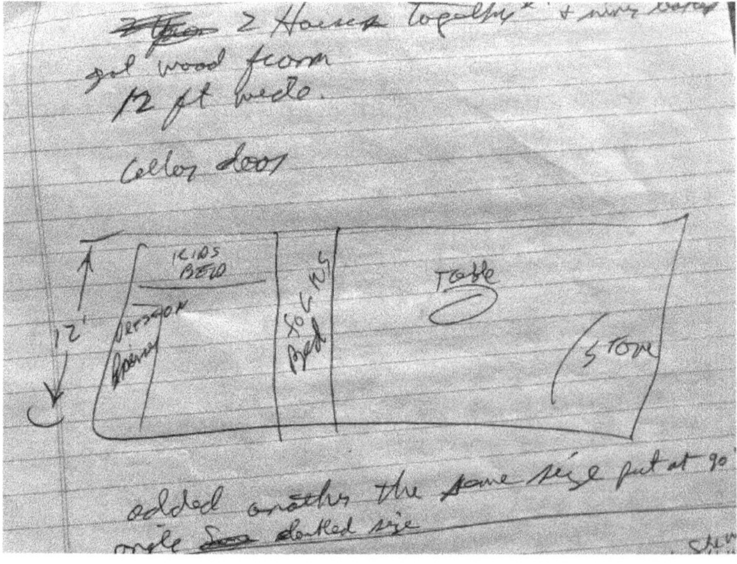

(Photo of sketch on my notepad as Joyce was describing their family shack.)

This ends my notes of Joyce reminiscing of the old times.

We lived in Grant until 1908—trying to clear a piece of land, but the years were wet.

Finally, Gertie, my wife, got sick and the doctor advised me to move to some different climate as she had tuberculosis, but, if we would go in time, she might get over it. So we decided to go west.

Wietze, my brother, and Martin Van Duine, a brother-in-law, started for Chicago.

We read an ad in the paper that on a certain date an excursion left for the west.

So, while in Holland, Michigan, my uncle, William Wilterdink, told us that John Rooks was an agent for a certain land company in Lemmon, South Dakota, and was making trips to the west to locate people on homestead land in western South Dakota.

So, we sent for and got John Rooks to go with us (where) we took the boat to Chicago and the train to Lemmon, South Dakota. All three of us (Wietze, Martin, and me) took up homesteads in what is now called Holland Center. The church now stands joining the three homesteads.

When we got back to Grant (Michigan), one of our neighbors, Mr. Marinus Van Wyk, asked us if we had found and filed on land. We told him we did. So he said he was going to go with us as soon as we were moving there. He said he would hold a (moving) sale the same day as we did (though he) did not have very much to sell.

I advised him not to do this as we thought it would be better for him to go and look for himself first, rather than take our word of it. But, he said he was going to sell out and go with us.

So four families within a mile from each other took an immigrant (rail) car together and took a few pieces of furniture and bedding, a wagon and stoves, and what we could pack in a boxcar.

We billed the (box) car to Hettinger, North Dakota, our nearest railroad station which is about twenty-one miles from Holland Center.

So we visited in and around Holland and Graafschap (Michigan) for a few days where the relatives lived. My wife's parents were still living at Graafschap yet.

The latter part of July 1908 we took the boat to Chicago and from there we took the train to Hettinger, North Dakota.

When we arrived in Hettinger, we sent word to the Le Febres.

Dick, John and Fred Le Febre, who also had filed on land east of Holland Center (SD), as they promised us, they would haul the furniture and what other stuff we had in the (box) car.

Of course it took some time to get word to the Le Febres as there were no telephones. (There was) not even a road from Holland Center to Lodgepole (SD) just a trail across the prairie. So, we stayed in Hettinger about four days. Then, the Le Febres came and we loaded up furniture and some lumber for the sod house.

The family, too, had to go along with the outfit (freight wagon), (as) we started out on our way to our claims.

We had not gotten very far and the tires (wagon rims) started to come off from the wheels as it was an old wagon and had dried out. So, every little while we had to stop and pound the tires on but finally got to our claim.

We made what shelter we could out of the few boards we had on the wagon. We had no mattress and as the prairie had been pastured off so close by the sheep and cattle of the ranchers such that we could not pick up enough grass to make up any bedding. So, we just had to lay on the ground with what bedding we had over us.

We started to build sod houses. It took about nine days to build our sod house.

The first Sunday we were there, Fred, John and Dick Le Febre came and Fred read a sermon. After the service we had a shower of rain.

We had an umbrella and I and my wife held that above us. The children, Henry, Gertie[6], Will, and John sat under the table.

---

[6] Gertie was the mother of Joyce Dole-Anderson.

The shelter we put up was nothing but boards up and down—more for a shelter from the sun than anything else.

You will probably wonder where Annie and Jennie were at that time.

Well, they got work in a hotel in Lemmon, South Dakota, so they were not with us (in) what at the time was our home-sweet-home.

Chapter 4E[7]

Explanation and Details

(by Gary W. Wietgrefe)

The original Beld family of Dutch heritage emigrated from Bentheim, which is a county of Lower Saxony, Germany on the eastern border of The Netherlands approximately eighty miles east of Amsterdam. They spoke Low German with Dutch influence.

The emigrating mother's family was from Gronegan, now written Groningan, a city and province bordering the North Sea in northeast Netherlands. It is approximately a hundred miles northeast of Amsterdam and a hundred miles west of Bremen, Germany.

In the 1800s, it was common for European emigrants to settle at similar latitudes and climate conditions in the U.S. This author's maternal grandfather emigrated in 1911 from South Russia (now Ukraine) to northcentral South Dakota. Interestingly, my grandparents

---

[7] Chapter number followed by "E" is an explanation to the chapter.

settled approximately a hundred and twenty miles east and at about the same latitude as the Beld family.

Amsterdam, Netherlands, however, is about fifty-two degrees North latitude compared to Grand Rapids, Michigan at forty-two degrees North, but Grand Rapids gets about six more inches of precipitation a year than Amsterdam.

As homesteader John Beld explained, he was hired (six years employed) as a machinist helper and staining at a furniture manufacturer, but likely he felt he could better his finances for his growing family by working for himself as a farmer.

The move to a Grant, Michigan farm was settled many years earlier and obviously on timber ground with drainage problems that was "low…and no good outlet for water (with) stumps and rotting logs."

Farming is always a delicate balance between timely rains to produce crops with ground not too wet to plant and harvest, and not too dry to prevent crop growth.

After struggling with water management, free homestead land and the lure for a dry farm in South Dakota likely sounded enticing. His wife Gertie's tuberculosis further motivated their move.

A dryland homestead was likely much drier than John Beld expected.

Lodgepole, South Dakota only gets an average of 15.2 inches of precipitation per year. That's less than half of Amsterdam and twenty-four inches less than Grant, Michigan.

May is generally the wettest month in Lodgepole which is why they likely planned to not bring mattresses from Michigan with the plan to fill bedding with grass in their original sod house.

Furthermore, homestead ground was never fenced. Previous settlers, cattle ranchers and sheep herders, had obviously taken advantage of free grazing on the unfenced Beld homestead.

Prairie hay, harvested in June for winter feed, was not an option on Beld's homestead in 1908. Dry years, which are often, prairie buffalo grass, which is nutritious for cattle, was likely the primary grass, but it only reaches a maximum height of about six inches. It would have been too short for cutting by scythe or horse-drawn mower.

Arriving "the later part of July," would have also been too late to plant crops or even a garden. Given four families packing their belongings in one railroad boxcar, meant that food supplies, like jars of vegetables and fruit, cured pork and beef, and bags of flour would have been limited.

There were many models of boxcars, but a typical railroad boxcar in 1908 was generally forty foot long, nine and a half foot wide, and ten foot internal height equaling approximately four thousand cubic feet which would be smaller than a typical two-car garage.

After arriving in Hettinger by rail, the Beld family was so short of money that their oldest two girls, Annie (just shy of her seventeenth birthday) and Jennie, age fifteen, were left in Lemmon, South Dakota to earn money. Likely, they were given room and board and a small wage.

Beld's homestead, a quarter-mile east of the Holland Center Christian Reformed Church, was approximately seven miles southwest of Lodgepole, Perkins County, South Dakota.

After waiting four days in Hettinger for the Le Febres's wagon to arrive, allowed time to purchase a few boards to use on Beld's sod house roof.

South Dakota state Highway 75 now runs north/south through Lodgepole south to Highway 20 (west of Bison) and north of Lodgepole to the North Dakota border where it changes to North Dakota Highway 8 into Hettinger. Likely, a wagon path existed from the Hettinger railhead to Lodgepole.

Le Febres' wagon problems were likely expected, since it was "an old wagon." What multiplied the problem was the wooden wagon wheel spokes "had dried out."

Wagon wheels are structurally supported by often sixteen to twenty-four spokes imbedded in the outside wooden support rim and center wooden hub.

In the 1990s, this author refurbished a well-cared for triple-box wagon. The rim and hub were oiled at least annually but wet rot, dry rot, and humidity changes made it difficult to keep the wagon wheels in operable condition.

Rail travel sped the drying process. Moving a wooden wagon and furniture from Michigan to western South Dakota would have quickly loosened the wagon box, frame, and especially the wagon wheels.

Why?

Average humidity in Grand Rapids, Michigan in July is about seventy percent. Whereas Hettinger, ND humidity in July is often under forty percent, often under twenty percent with hot northwesterly winds.

Consequently, wooden wagon wheels likely dried out in boxcar transit and dried further after arriving in the Dakotas.

Besides being an old wagon, the drop in humidity likely caused wood shrinkage of wheel rungs and hubs, "so every little while we had to stop and pound the tires on."

Maintaining their Christian religion was very important to homesteading families, especially the John and Wietze Beld's, Martin Van Duine, Marinus Van Wyk, and the three Le Febre (Fred, John and Dick).

The Holland Center Christian Reformed Church, which still stands today, was located at the intersection of three homesteads.

Beld's daughters, Annie and Jennie, were in Lemmon, South Dakota approximately thirty miles across virgin, unmarked prairie as the crow flies from Beld's sod house.

Teenagers worked to earn money for themselves and help their family make ends meet. No school loans nor credit cards were available.

Banks provided loans based on the integrity of the borrower and assets. In that parched land, equipment could be valuable for someone in need or worthless during droughts. Banks were businessmen and leery. There were no federal or state programs to guarantee loans.

Chapter 5

Pocket book empty

(By John Beld)

So, we were busy building our sod house, but as our pocket book was empty, we could not put in a floor, nor door, and got along without a door until fall.

I kept busy building houses for John and Dick Le Febre and earned enough money to buy lumber for a floor and a door by the time we were getting cold weather.

I told John Rooks, who was living in Lemmon, to try and get work for me in Lemmon.

He got me a job digging a basement for a saloon. This took quite a while as the ground was frozen.

When that was finished, I got a job digging a cistern and cellar for a banker. Then, I helped build a house with the Voight boys.

This house that I helped build was for C.D. Smith. So, after we had the house built, C.D. Smith wanted to build a fence around his lot and put in his garden and plant trees on his lot.

Mr. Smith asked me to come and work for him doing the janitor work and running the electric light plant.

I asked him what kind of electric light plant he had. He said it was a gas engine and dynamo.

I told him I was pretty well posted in running steam engines but not running a gas engine and dynamo and thought he better keep the man he had. But, he did not take care of it as he would get drunk. If I was a steam engineer, and he had the books, I would get along with it o.k.

By this time, it was June and I received word that Wietze's wife was very sick and to come home. So, I took the train to Hettinger. I asked the doctor how she was. He said she was dead and he expected they would be in Hettinger with her body.

Wietze's wife had given birth to their sixth child just two weeks before her death. The baby stayed with sister Jane Van Duine, as they had a cow and could provide milk for baby Gerrit.

Wietze's wife was going to be buried in Michigan where three of their infants were buried before. So, I decided my brother needed me to go with him, so when he came with the body and the little girls, I went with him to Holland, Michigan. There the little girls stayed with their grandparents, the Hesselinks.

We stayed there a few days, then visiting the relatives, before going back to Dakota.

This was the latter part of July. Wietze and I decided to go with the threshing crew to earn money to get started as there was a poor crop, so not much feed for the cattle we now had.

After threshing was finished, Wietze got work in Montana and I went back to work in Lemmon where our girls Annie and Jennie were working in the hotel.

We did not get to go to our home to see the rest of the family very often. They managed as best they could with the little we had.

End of John Beld's writing.

Chapter 5E

Explanation and Details

(By Gary W. Wietgrefe)

Lack of money can cause strain on any family. To find income the father living separately magnified the problem. An infant death made tragedy.

On the homestead, or hired, work was hard. Imagine spending weeks digging a basement in frozen dirt with a pick, crowbar and shovel.

There were seven children in our family; six going to school; and farm income (split with my grandfather) did not allow my father to stay home during the week. South Dakota, covered in snow did not stop construction.

One winter my father was on a well-drilling crew. Miserable work. For years, until he was forced to retire in his late forties due to heart problems, he worked nine-hour days for a local lumber yard on steel and wood construction throughout the hot 100+°F summers and minus 20°F miserably cold winters.

Farming over a thousand acres, running a herd of beef cattle, a dairy, raising hogs, producing spring wheat, oats, barley, rye, flax, millet, corn, cane, alfalfa, cutting prairie hay, and raising a family of seven children was my father and mother's full-time jobs.

No matter how mother patched and acquired hand-me-downs from our cousins, we needed clothes and shoes for school. John Beld and his wife did the same fifty years earlier for his family.

Like my father who brought home used, twisted, and scrap lumber for barn and fence repair, John Beld, worked over thirty miles from his family's homestead in order to put a floor over dirt in their sod shanty.

No doubt his wife Gertie kept a clean house, likely requiring the children to sweep the dirt floor daily.

However, standing and sleeping on dirt, summer or winter is not sanitary even when the chamber pot was carried to the outhouse early each morning.

A layer of wood above the dirt would make the sod-sided home warmer and cleaner.

Obviously, successfully digging a basement led to more digging. Before farms or towns had running water in their homes, water had to be carried into the house, or snow and ice melted in winter for drinking, cooking, cleaning, and laundry. Many towns existed decades before a centralized water tower and gravity system of pipes delivered water to homes.

Just because a city invested in a water system didn't mean it connected to every home. Why not? It cost money.

For example, when I was a child we would visit my mother's grandmother (my maternal great grandmother) in Selby, South Dakota. Selby, a railroad community approximately a hundred and fifty miles east of Lodgepole, erected the city's first water tower in 1894. Into the mid-1960s I remember being scolded, "Stay off the cistern" for fear that one of us children would fall in and drowned.

In the 1970s, I asked my mother why great Grandma Wagner, who lived across the street from the Walworth County Courthouse, relied on cistern water? My mother responded immediately, "They could not afford to pay for city water."

Homesteaders and city residents first used wooden rain barrels (which held about fifty gallons) to catch water from house and barn roofs, but water would freeze in winter and get mossy and algae infested in summer.

A water cistern, holding thirty or so barrels, allowed for a larger, healthier water supply close to the house. (Remember water for John and Gertie's sod shanty had to be carried a mile and a half before a cistern or well was dug.)

John was also hired to dig a cellar—often called a root cellar which had two primary purposes. First, it was a place to store food, canned (in jars), garden produce (especially root crops like potatoes, carrots, beets, turnips), but also winter melons and fruits (like apples and covered green tomatoes that ripened slowly).

Secondly, cellars were used as an emergency shelter from tornados, cyclone winds, blizzards, and hailstorms.

Keep in mind, sod homes like the Beld's were replaced with the first wooden homes often without insulation. Siding and roofs were generally covered only with cheap tarpaper.

Until I was five years old, our family (then with five children) lived in the 18' foot by 20 foot, three room, one bedroom tarpapered shack.

Constructed on the prairie, usually anticipating where a railroad would be built, the small, flimsy structures often were mounted on two parallel beams, so they could be easily moved if the railroad located elsewhere.

Not anchored, those homes, shops, or one-room schools could easily blow over or apart during a major windstorm. Settlers soon learned such windstorms bringing baking summer heat or winter blizzards were common on the Dakota Plains.

Labor, especially skilled labor, was in short supply in pioneering days. It still is. Ask any farmer, rancher, or rural businessperson if they can readily hire local skilled labor in 2026? The universal answer over a century since the last homesteaders is a resounding "NO!"

Labor-saving technology, like electricity and gas-powered motors, were readily adopted in the Dakota prairies.

When John Beld was asked if he could be hired as the home's gas-powered electric plant and dynamo operator, he declined because he honestly did not have experience with gasoline motors.

Where John lacked skills, he had ample work ethic, was literate, and not a drunkard.

Mr. C.D. Smith replied, "…If you were a steam engineer and he had the books…" (meaning the gas motor and dynamo's operating manual), "you would get along o.k."

John's brother, Wietze, lost his wife following childbirth. What made it more tragic, they had left three infants buried in Michigan. No wonder his wife preferred to be buried there rather than in a remote South Dakota cemetery. Likely, in those early years there was no cemetery.

To support his brother, John took what little money he had to accompany his brother and dead sister-in-law for burial in Michigan.

Upon return in late July, oats (horse feed), barley (cattle and hog feed), and hard red spring wheat (for baking flour), on good years was ready to harvest.

By the early 1900s prairie farmers no longer used a scythe to cut grain. Cyrus McCormick's grain reaper, invented in 1831, and Andrew Meikle's threshing machine invented fifty years earlier (1786), were quickly adopted as labor-saving farm harvesting machinery.

However, reapers bound bundles of grain that had to be shocked (often eight bundles leaned together upright to dry the heads of grain). Those bundles, after drying a week or more, had to be loaded on hay wagons and hauled to a threshing machine conveniently centralized in customary forty-acre fields.

I learned from my father to shock grain and watched him throw bundles on our horse-drawn wagon which were delivered to our threshing machine. At first my job was to keep our water jug in the shade and to keep threshed oats from going over the sides of our wooden wagon.

Until the end of World War II (1945), threshing machines were too expensive for one farmer. Often a wealthy farmer, or a group of farmers (usually brothers) would invest in a threshing machine and move from crop-to-crop, field-to-field, farm-to-farm, to harvest various grains.

Though threshing crews efficiently operated with eight or more men, during WWI and WWII with men up to forty gone to war, threshing crews often consisted of old men, and teenage boys and girls.

My mother, ages twelve to fourteen, had to quit school during WWII to help on their Walworth County threshing crew.

After WWII portable grain combines (combined reaping and threshing grain) were quickly adopted—mainly because they required about eighty percent less labor.

My disabled paternal grandfather bought a new threshing machine after WWII when iron again became available. He thought he made a wise financial deal, but my father had to quit school at age fourteen to run the thresh machine, by himself or with his aging WWI and WWII uncles.

My first harvest, I was likely four years old. A day or so before, dad had used our 1947 H-International tractor and pulled our horse-drawn grain binder which accumulated and dumped eight bundles of grain in straight rows on fresh-cut, golden stubble.

During shocking each bundle was picked up, grain heads to the top, and bunched eight per shock. I would tote our gallon glass vinegar jug from shock-to-shock covered in blue jean patches to keep it cool. My only other job was to remember which shock I put it in—all shocks looked the same.

A week or so later, after the grain in shocks dried, I would ride the bundle wagon to pick up the bundles.

Dad would click his tongue as a signal for the horses to move forward and say "Whoa" for them to stop at the next shock. Once the load was filled as high as my father could throw bundles with a three-tined bundle fork, Lady and Babe, our draft horses, would walk to the threshing machine.

Too dangerous to be anywhere close to the contraption of gears, rollers, belts, chains, and feeder bars, my threshing job was to keep oats from going over the sides of our triple-box wooden wagon. Yes, oats was the first crop harvested in the season, and thereby my first job on the two person threshing crew.

Was my father counting on his four-year-old to help harvest, or was he training me to farm? Likely both.

The 1909 grain crop was scant in Perkins County prompting John to accompany Wietze, his brother, on a North Dakota threshing crew. Also, notable is that John had earned enough money to get some cows—several which were milked for household use and cream sales in Lodgepole.

In that part of South Dakota, pasture grass often is too short for grazing by October. Six months of cattle feed, hay, whatever was cut and stacked had to last until at least April when pastures greened into spring.

Chapter 6

Memories and Beld Family Research

(As written in 1984 by seventy-two-year-old Grace Albertha Beld-Vander Zeen with family support.)

The author and compiler of these records and history is Grace, (photo left) the eighth child of John and Gertrude Beld. (At date of publication) she lives in Ripon, California where also her family live. Her husband, Gerald Vander Veen, was an almond farmer until his death in 1960.

Grace and Gerald worked together as a team and raised four children whom they loved and taught the "fear of the Lord."

Grace is retired and lives in Ripon where she enjoys her hobbies and her family. The Senior Citizens are a big pastime to her. She has many, many friends and is a member of the First Christian Reformed Church. This book was printed in June 1984.

The youngest daughter of John and Gertie, Grace, was born in Lemmon, South Dakota, February 26, 1912. It has been a pleasure to learn so much about my father's family and background.

I really did not think we would ever get it all together and without cousin George Beld's help and encouragement to keep at it, I think I would have given up.

It really was my father's idea to do this. He used to say so often, "Why don't you write for the information of each family and get to them to fill you in with what each one remembers of the things happening in their families, or what was told them by their father and mother?"

Well, I did try to get them to do just that. But, they had excuses galore. So the information I got was mostly by visits and one faithful letter writer, George Beld, who really went all out to get this finished.

But now it is ten years later and George Beld too has gone home to be with the Lord.

Most of this material was compiled in 1969. We sincerely regret that it was not ready to be published five years earlier. There is still so much that is not complete. Rather than wait any longer, we have decided to get it out.

It is a fulfillment of the desire expressed by many of them that the story be written so later generations might know more about the Belds' migration and early life in America.

It should be of interest to all of us of later generations to know about the religious and economic forces which caused our forefathers to come to this land of promise.

We wish to thank those who have helped in collecting this information. Those who wrote portions of this booklet have been named with their material. Space does not permit listing all the others, but their help is appreciated.

May the Belds of the future look back with respect and gratitude to the spirit and determination of our forefathers.

In our daily lives, may our attitude toward God and our fellow man exemplify our heritage which we owe to Hendrick Jan Beld and his wife Anje Belo-Bos-Beld.

Since I am the caboose of the family, it was mostly here say, but I was a good listener and enjoyed hearing my brothers and sisters talk about the olden days in Michigan where they all were born.

Anyway, our father did write his part up to my birth. Then somehow, he expected me to go on from there.

Well, I'll give you my father's story.

A family picture (below) of our grandparents, Henry John Beld and Anje Belo-Bos-Beld was possibly taken in 1887 before the birth of Grace Mina Beld who was born June 22, 1887.

Grandfather Henry John Beld died April 18, 1889. The Children in this picture are:

John Harm Beld born February 23, 1867
John Beld born July 25, 1870
Jane Beld born October 11, 1872
Chynthia Beld born September 12, 1875
Wietze Beld born November 29, 1877
Henry John Beld born September 6, 1881
Anna Beld born June 3, 1884

Grandmother Anje Beld married again March 25, 1891 and another daughter was born: Marie Glerum born

November 13, 1895. Grandmother Beld-Blerum died December 1, 1895.

(Note: About a century before the Belds moved to South Dakota, the camera was invented. Before photography, pencil sketches were made—usually of important people. The big box stationary cameras standing on tripod legs made images on glass plates. The Belds, like many families, saved money, put on their best church clothes and went to a bigger town that had a photographer to have a family photo taken. Photographing a family was a serious occasion. It was not proper back then to smile.)

Chapter 7

Gertie Heetderks-Beld Moves Forward

(By Grace Beld-Vander Veen)

Now (after my father's story ends), my mother, Gertie Heetderks-Beld, had little Gerrit, the baby of Uncle Wietze and Aunt Anna. This was quite an experience, too. He got sick and being they were thirty miles from a doctor, their only way to explain how sick he was was by mail and waiting for an answer.

His pneumonia settled on his leg. The doctor wrote he'd come to lance it when it was ripe, which he did and Gerrit became well and healthy again. But, his leg always stayed shorter and so he stayed crippled.

I'm sure those days of sickness and no conveniences put extra hardships on mother. Being she knew the Lord, she went to Him with all her troubles.

Mother was thankful her health was returning. Although she was not ever very strong, she was able to manage the family affairs without our father while he worked in Lemmon.

Gertie[8] was sixteen and Henry fourteen with the other two boys being eight and six.

School was far from their little sod shanty and one teacher taught all eight grades.

Well, by now it was 1911 and another poor crop with winter coming and a baby expected in February of 1912. So, our father tried to get a house in Lemmon and move the family there for the winter.

There was not much to be gotten, but a small shack on the outskirts of Lemmon. They moved there with their cattle and all they needed to survive the winter. So the family could be together. There were some sputterings about a new baby to arrive which added burden on the family.

(With the children having to move, change schools, and join their older sisters) mother had to do some explaining, disciplining and finally all was straightened out again and forgiven.

Then, it happened on the cold Sunday evening. Mother became sick and told Ann to send her boyfriend home and for him to tell our father to come home with the doctor.

Ann's boyfriend left his fur coat to cover mother in bed and went as he was bid to do.

---

[8] At age sixteen, Gerdie, mother of Joyce Dole-Anderson, walked thirty to thirty-five miles in one day in the spring of 1912 to their homestead seven miles southwest of Lodgepole.

Our father and the doctor came and I was born that Monday morning, February 26, 1912, when it was twenty-eight degrees below zero.

When the winter was over and the weather straightened out, they went back to the sod house on the prairie and started farming again.

Just when our father gave up his job of night watch and janitorial work in Lemmon, South Dakota, I don't know when. But, the girls (Annie and Jennie) gave up their jobs too to live on their claims as that was a requirement.

Church life continued in the vacant sod house of Uncle Wietze as he was still in Montana. He had married Lucy Weidenaar, December 29, 1912, and settle there.

At the time, there were other Holland folks living west of the (Holland Center Christian Reformed) Church. Uncle Martin Van Duines, Belds, the Le Febres, Lubbers, Doles, the Vliem brothers, and also Van Wyks were getting together. That sounded good to them and they decided to come too on the next Sunday.

So, the church soon grew a little larger and this is the way Ann and Jennine (my sisters) found their mates.

These folks too, had filed on claims and were living there.

Ann married Peter Stuit an eligible young bachelor, and Jennie married Gerrit Vliem, also a young bachelor all within a few years. They settled down to live where their offspring still are living today (1983).

Chapter 7E

Explanation and Details

(By Gary W. Wietgrefe)

Just a few things to point out—proving a homestead claim, changing agricultural systems, and finding mates.

There are six hundred and forty acres to a section of land as gridded across the U.S. Each section is divided into four quarter sections of a hundred and sixty acres each. Each quarter section is subdivided into "eighties" and eighties divided into "forties." A South Dakota Homestead was a hundred and sixty acres.

The Homestead Act signed by President Abraham Lincoln, May 20, 1862, allowed U.S. citizens, Reservation Indians, and potential citizens to claim a homestead. It required three things:

1. File and application and pay $1.25 per acre.
2. Improve the land (including a home).
3. After five years, pay another small fee to file for a deed for title (called a land patent).

Using horses to plow, seed, cultivate, and harvest, to have reasonably managed grain field sizes, Dakota prairie pioneers often broke (plowed) fields segregated into forty acres. A home, usually a sod shanty, was considered an improvement as was tilling ground to plant crops, putting in fences, corrals and barns for livestock.

By 1934 ten percent of the U.S., 270 million acres of America's frontier, was mainly in the territories of the Louisiana Purchase. In 1976 the Homestead Act of 1862 was repealed, except granting Alaska development another decade.

After the passing of my parents, I owned Edmunds County Land (200 miles due east of Beld's homestead) that was homesteaded in 1884. Historically, homesteading in the Plains progressed east to west primarily following moisture patterns from higher to lower precipitation.

The first Wietgrefes arrived in South Dakota in 1905—three years before the Belds.

My great grandfather, Henry (H.L.) Wietgrefe emigrated from the Hannover area of Germany with his parents to eastern Iowa in 1869. Married, with a growing family of six children, H.L. decided eastern Iowa was not the best place to raise cattle.

H.L. was so poor he couldn't afford train fare.

So, in the spring of 1905, H.L. with his son Walter (my grandfather age 13) and his brother Henry (age 12) drove their meager herd of cattle over five hundred miles to the first Wietgrefe farm in northcentral South Dakota.[9]

At the time, the Ipswich area was grassland and cattle country with few fences and few wheat fields. Brown County, the next county east, was where large-scale wheat production ended. Cattle became the primary farm revenue source west of the Wietgrefe farm.

In fact, although my Ipswich, SD ground was homesteaded in 1884, it was grassland cut for hay. It was not fenced until my father owned and fenced it in the late 1940s. That ground remained pasture until 1999 when my mother, then a widower, had sold all her cattle and allowed our tenant neighbor to farm that virgin sod without tilling the soil.

Before no-tillage management, a ton per acre grass or one cow/calf pair on ten acres was the expected production. To make the Ipswich area agronomically sound over the long-haul more crops should be rotated, but our area now only produces corn and soybeans. Let me briefly explain how and when South Dakota agriculture fundamentally changed after 2000.

Based on a thirty-year average, our farm southwest of Ipswich, SD gets just over three more inches of precipitation per year (18.4 in/yr) than Lodgepole, SD (15.2 in/yr.). The old farmer's term is "rain makes grain."

---

[9] My books, Lesson of an Immigrant Father--1905 cattle drive 500 miles to Dakota, details the cattle drive of my great grandfather, grandfather, and great uncle.

Montana State University claims it takes five inches of moisture to produce one bushel of wheat. Each additional inch can produce seven more bushels. How can available moisture be conserved?

A farming rule of thumb is that one inch of moisture evaporates each tillage trip.

Homesteaders a century ago through the 1980s tilled ground three to five times each year to control weeds and provide a planting seedbed. Result: Dust storms.

United States Department of Agriculture has been reporting South Dakota average wheat yields since 1879. South Dakota wheat yield averages select decades include Beld's homesteading era: 1879-1888 = 11.6 bushels/acre; 1908-1917 = 10.8 bu/ac; 1930-1939 = 7.6 bu/ac; 1970-1979 = 22.9 bu/ac; and 2016-2025 = 46.7 bu/ac.

What changed?

Moisture? Sure. Decade average moisture fluctuates but that is not the driving factor.

Improved wheat breeding?

Sure. Wheat varieties have improved somewhat, but that does not explain yields differences. Varietal selection and university breeding programs have been going on since the Civil War and extensively through the 1970s but plant breeding did not change the yield trend.

Pest control?

Sure. Weed pests, insects, and disease control products have been commercialized during the twentieth century, but they do not add one bushel to yield.

A common mistake farmers and agronomists make is by promoting how a variety, nutrient, or better pest control product increases yield. They do not.

The way to correctly address the topic is—does the change help the plant reach its potential yield.

What changed South Dakota wheat yields (11.6 to 46.7 bushels per acre) between 1879 and 2025?

Two things: West movement and moisture.

Homesteaders moved west planting wheat from highest moisture parts of South Dakota on the Minnesota border in the 1870s to the Wyoming border by 1910.

Homesteaders always planted their most fertile ground to wheat. Thereby, in the first decades, they benefited from centuries of nature's trapped bio-carbon and nutrients.

As an agronomist, I'm convinced the biggest factor is no-tillage wheat production. The program I introduced in the mid-1980s started with wheat, corn, sorghum, and millet rotations in commercial sized fields from Agar to Pierre, south to Ideal, Hamill, Chamberlain and east to Wessington.

The program of conserving moisture and minimizing erosion was so successful that those acres phased out of wheat in favor of higher revenue crops/higher moisture utilizing crops like corn and soybeans.

To teach benefits of the system to other farmers, some of my trial farmers from 1985-1990 cooperated with South Dakota State University to form the Dakota Lakes Research Farm near Pierre, South Dakota in 1990.

To this day thirty-six years later, Dakota Lakes Research Farm shows how farmers can take advantage of no-till research to improve profitability on their farms.

Homesteaders, with scant knowledge of research, tended to rely on farming knowledge passed from generation to generation. However, what provided good yields in higher moisture areas of Europe and Michigan were seldom the same plant varieties or techniques that worked in arid western South Dakota.

Even into the mid-1980s, a year of wheat followed by a year of fallow and another year of wheat in central and western South Dakota was the standard practice.

Rather than getting one crop every two years (wheat followed by fallow), farmers saved time and moisture not tilling. Result: Since 1990 farmers have been harvesting continuous crops (wheat, corn, soybeans, sorghum, sunflowers, and millet) on the same "wheat ground" every year which multiplied their income significantly from several crops including increased wheat yields.

Initially, it took more pesticides to control weeds, but by not tilling through year five pesticide use decreased and natures' balance of organic matter and the soil's biodiversity were beginning to be restored.

Hence: 1970s wheat yields of 22.9 bushels per acre more than doubled to 46.7 bushels per acre from 2016-2025 utilizing no-tillage practices (often called regenerative agriculture) even as wheat acreages continued to move west into lower precipitation areas.

Moisture conserved year-around allowed high-moisture utilizing crops, like corn and soybeans, to replace wheat in eastern and central South Dakota.

Currently, most of South Dakota wheat is produced west of the Missouri River on only fifteen to seventeen inches of annual precipitation.

Money supply generates farm prosperity.

The world-wide economic depression in the 1890s slowed Dakota homesteading. The 1930s economic depression coincided with the multi-year drought in the U.S. Plains. Tens of thousands of farms and ranches, including homesteads were lost by government confiscation for unpaid property taxes.

As a trained economist, I look back on that era of fundamental economic flaws. While the federal, state, and local governments desired to keep families on their farms, each government layer tightened farm and consumer money supply, called M1[10], such that normal economic activity was unsustainable.

Federal work programs [Civilian Conservation Corp (CCC), Work Progress Administration (WPA)], state, county, and township road, bridge, and dam building employed desperate laborers at a dollar per day which did not inject dollars into local economies. Such low family income was not sustainable.

In fact, as you will read later, government at all levels, pulled money and labor out of farm, ranch and businesses at every administrative level. It was just the opposite of economic stimulus.

Though Annie and Jennie worked mostly in Lemmon during the initial years, in the spring of 1912 when the family left winter quarters outside of Lemmon, the family, including the two oldest girls move to their 160-acre homestead claims. That allowed the family to homestead three adjoining quarter sections (480 acres) using the remain two summers to "prove-up" their claims.

Finding a spouse was not the easiest, especially for young men who primarily made homestead claims, or accompanied their family to prove-up claims.

---

[10] M1 is a term designating the supply of currency readily available to spend from cash, bank check, savings, and CD accounts.

Since many areas of the U.S. were settled by ethnic groups, often affiliated by religion, the most likely place to attract a spouse was at church.

Given the distance between homesteads, the lack of roads, and convenient transportation, churches served not only a religious function, but especially Sundays served as a social function. As mentioned, that is how Annie and Jennie found mates and likely found help to prove and maintain their land claims.

Moving west was a common pioneer theme. The girls grandparents, Henry John Beld and Anje Bos-Beld, had moved west from Europe (Germany and Holland) to Michigan. Their children, John and Gertie, moved west to South Dakota from Michigan all while maintaining their religious convictions.

"We Three Kings," the first Christian hymn written in the U.S. by John Henry Hopkins in 1857, was likely a popular Christmas carol for pioneers, like the Belds. With the chorus repeated enthusiastically every five lines:

O Star of Wonder, Star of Night,
Star with Royal Beauty bright,
Westward leading,
Still proceeding,
Guide us to Thy perfect Light.

Chapter 8

Hint of Success

(By Grace Beld-Vander Veen)

When the Dakotas are blessed with rain, crops are good and farmers make a good living. They raise cattle, sheep, and put up plenty of feed to take care of their stock through the winter, which are usually cold with lots of snow.

They don't complain and are quite content to be Dakotans.

Our father didn't mention the Farmers Cooperative Creamery which was quite a successful operation. For years, he was president.

The creamery was still in operation in 1934 when I got married. When it closed its doors, I don't know.

I think he should have mentioned the creamery as it was one of his stories he liked to tell, how it came into being, etc.

The Creamery was located in Lodgepole (seven miles from where we lived). In Lodgepole, there also was a store (now run by grandson of Gerrit and Jennie Vliem, and the post office was run by Le Febre, also a grandson of the pioneers).

Sister, Gertie[11], also married a son of the pioneers, Martin Dole, who settled there until 1948. Their oldest daughter, Joyce, married a pioneer's son, George Anderson, and they still live in South Dakota.

Brother, William, married a New Holland girl and lived there until 1945. Brother John Jr. married a Harrison, South Dakota[12] girl and lived at Holland Center (having bought the Van Duine place). They lived there until they retired in Hettinger, North Dakota.

I, Grace, am the last one to be born and lived in Dakota until 1934 when I married a fellow from Corsica, South Dakota. We moved to California on our honeymoon and that is where I still live.

Mother, Gertie Heetderks-Beld, died April 19, 1944, at Holland Center. Father, John Beld, died August 20, 1961, at Artesia, California. Both are buried at Holland Center.

Their children are:

Annie Beld-Stuit born September 19, 1891;
Jennie Beld-Vliem born May 5, 1893, died April 30, 1928.

---

[11] Gertie was Joyce Anderson's mother.

[12] Belds moved from Holland, Michigan to Holland Center, SD which is in Perkins County. New Holland and Harrison, SD are small Douglas County (east-river) communities between Platte and Corsica. Harrison Reformed Church is still in Harrison.

Gertie Beld-Dole born June 3, 1895, died January 23, 1981.
Henry John Beld born March 29, 1897, died Oct. 17, 1918.
William Beld born September 21, 1899, died Sep. 23, 1899.
William Beld born September 19, 1901, died Feb. 26, 1983.
John Beld Jr. born August 17, 1903, died Jan. 18, 1980.
Grace Albetha Beld-Vander Veen born, February 26, 1912.

The occasion of this family photo was when my father and Uncle Wietze brought my Aunt Anna's body and their daughters to Michigan in 1911. Front row (L-R): Aunt Grace and Uncle Albert Wilterdink holding baby Grace; then in the background are the parents of Uncle Albert Wilterdink, Gesia Mul and Wilm Oom.

Chapter 9

Grandparent Memories

(By Grace Beld-Vander Veen)

Now some of the things I (Grace) remember my parents talking about that Pa didn't mention was the death of his father in 1889 and the death of Uncle John Harm's bride of eight months.

After our grandfather's (Henry John Beld) death, grandma Anji Bos-Beld wanted my father and mother (John and Gertie-Heetderks-Beld) to get married and stay with her on the farm. They did and lived in a house on the yard until grandma got married again to Jacob Glerum.

Great grandfather Belds home near Zeeland, Michigan

Grandma Beld had a big house and it was very clean. She loved beautiful flowers and houseplants. (Photo circa 1970s?)

She was also a good seamstress and made all of her own and her girls' dresses as well as underclothes.

Grandmother Beld's brother was an auctioneer.

After Grandma Beld married again, they didn't need to live near (John's mother) grandma anymore. So, they moved to Wayland, Michigan where Ann was born.

Great grandfathers barn
This barn goes with the red brick home.

Father and mother often talked about the dog, too. It was trained to keep the churn going that made the butter.

Grandmother Beld had quite a time with the parents of Grandpa Beld. As they got very old, great grandmother became unwilling to cooperate.

As far as washing clothes went, she took clean clothes out of the chest of drawers and hung them on the line rather than change clothes. So it didn't take long to find this out. Lice were found on her body.

After this closer watch was needed, life became a bit more hectic.

These great grandparents lived a long life together. I think we children all remember hearing our father saying that his grandparents, who were responsible for all the Belds in America, often bragged about how they had eaten Easter eggs together for sixty years.

Old grandmother was happy when she had wool to spin and a spinning wheel.

She died at the age of eighty-eight. Great grandfather died at the age of ninety-six.

Chapter 10

Oldest Living Granddaughter

(By Grace Beld-Vander Veen)

This story is being made as a memorial to the oldest living granddaughter of Henry John and Anje Bos-Beld. Annie Beld-Stuit is 92 and living in Hettinger, North Dakota in the Hillcrest Care Center.

Her voice on the tape is as clear as a bell and her mind was then too on their fiftieth wedding anniversary.

Since then, they've celebrated their 64th wedding anniversary and her voice is not so clear and mind not so sharp.

So, it is with great pleasure to honor her (my oldest sister) with this book.

(Annie photo May 1983.)

May the Belds of the future look back with respect and gratitude for the information and material found in this book.

Those who wanted to see this book published during the years of the 1960s in our family alone are father, John Beld, sister Gertie Dole, and brothers William and Jack Beld, as well as my dear husband Gerald Vander Veen.

The cousins, Betty Eesing, Mary Brink and George Beld, gathered their family histories along with those I could never contact.

The family history of each family is not complete in as far as beginning is concerned. So, I tried to fill in where I could from a tape recording I took of a conversation with my dear sister, Anna Beld Stuit and her husband, Pete.

Also, I have written what is remembered of conversations with my father, since he was so intent on having his written down.

He never thought there would be any trouble getting the lines together. (Little did he know about it.)

Of the oldest in the family, John Harm Beld, there is the least and there was a lot of history to be told. That we couldn't get, so the book is being published without it.

(Photo believed to be L-R: Standing: Henry John, John Harm; Sitting: Wietze and John Beld.)

Chapter 11

Mass Migrations

(By Grace Beld-Vander Veen)

The Beld Family History:

Mass migrations of history are often inspired by a deep soul-stirring urge to enlarge the horizons of life, both spiritually and economically. Or, they have been fostered by a will to either correct or escape what was considered a real, evil or injustice.

Abraham, in response to God's command, got himself out of Ur of the Chaldees. With his family and servants they went to the land that God told him. "I will show thee."

The crusaders of the 12th century, which embodied one of the greatest mass movements of history, costing thousands of lives, were also deeply religious. Their inception was born of the desire to redeem the Holy Land from the Infidel.

The Puritans and the Pilgrims, leaving homeland behind, set out under the most trying circumstances for a land where they could worship God as they pleased.

The migration of the Dutch to western Michigan in 1857 was led by the heroic and divinely inspired character, Reverend Albert Van Raalte. He ranks well up among the heroic population movements of history as far as purity of ideal is concerned.

Primarily, the Van Raalte group came to America to attain freedom of worship.

They could have compromised their principles and remained in peace and tranquility in their homeland.

The State church, from which they were succeeders, was beginning to make concessions. But, Van Raalte and his followers preferred the hardships and trials of a dangerous ocean voyage.

It would involve the Herculean tasks of building their homes in a wooded wilderness in a strange land rather than sacrificing any portion of their religious convictions which they held dearer than life itself.

Our great grandparents, the Belds, came to this country a year or two after the first Van Raalte group arrived.

We have reasons to believe that they too were inspired by the same ideals that influenced the decisions of the original Van Raalte group. They lived in a vicinity (in Germany) near the Dutch border where the succeeders, De Cock and Scholte, were active.

The courage and idealism of our great grandparents with their four young children to come to America gives tone and color to the entire Beld family.

As descendants of this sturdy God-fearing stock, we should be thankful to God for the inspiration and vision which turned their faces toward America.

We should be proud of this heritage and guard it well.

We should be active and zealous to keep alive the inspiring traditions of our family. For, in so doing, we carry over the Biblical injunction, "Honor they father and thy mother."

The Hervormde Kerk Reformed Church[13] at that time was governed by the State which brought about much dissatisfaction. The main argument was that the church government was political and aristocratic.

A spiritual revival swept through the country attempting to bring back the old time religion of Calvin's teachings.

To stamp out the revival, the State made laws forbidding crowds over twenty persons to gather.

De Cock would preach to larger numbers. He was often disturbed by mobs throwing stones.

---

[13] Hervornde Kerk Reformed Church, also known as the Dutch Reformed Church, was the most prominent Christian denomination in the Netherlands from the 1520s until 1930.

Many of the preachers were arrested, imprisoned, and required to pay heavy fines.

The succeeders took the name "Gereformecade Kerk" or "Afgescheiding."[14]

The troubles of the new congregations continued and finally Reverend Scholte took his followers to America to found a settlement in Pella, Iowa.

Reverend Van Raalte emigrated a few years later and founded Holland, Michigan.

Years later after the Van Raalte departure of 1846, in 1857 the Belds arrived in America.

The fact that the Belds were members of the churches of the Netherlands and that they spoke the Holland language brands them as Hollanders. We know that Zeeland was a part of the United Netherlands until the eighteenth century.

In the true sense of language determines nationality. A common language of a community of people is the chief factor in the origin of nationality and nations.

But, for some unknown reason, the Hollanders of Zeeland, on the fringe of the Netherlands, were annexed

---

[14] Not to be confused with Dr. Martin Luther's 1517 reformation separation from the Roman Catholic Church, the "Gereformecade Kerk" or "Afgescheiding" movement decentralized Dutch orthodox worship in the early 1800s, rather than ascribing to king or government led church administration.

to Hanover.[15] In no sense do the Belds in America spring from German nationality. For, they left Europe either before or at the time of the Prussian invasion. Of the Belds who remained in Europe, this does not hold true.

Very little is known of the old home in the Netherlands. Records show the old great grandmother Beld. She died at the age of eighty-eight on January 28, 1893. Great grandfather Beld died at the age of ninety-six on November 8, 1895.

Great grandfather, Henry John Beld, was born at Gemente Glenkamp on October 23, 1840. He came to the United States in October 1857.

Grandmother, Anje Bos-Beld, was born in 1848 and had her first birthday on the sail boat. She was born in Groningen, Netherlands.

Gemente Leens, her father and mother and brother Wietze also came to the United States in 1848.

Grandmother Bos's death was not recorded in the family Bible. Grandfather, Jan Bos, died August 4, 1886. Her brother, Wietze Bos, died August 19, 1872.

There is no record of the brothers and sisters of grandfather Henry John Beld, but we do remember our father and mother talking about Aunt Minnie (Mien Mui), Aunt Grace (Gesia Mui), and an uncle (Oom Tien), and

---

[15] Hanover, led by the royal House of Hannover, under British authority from October 1814 (part of the German Confederation states), relinquished control to Prussia in1866.

our grandfather, Henry John. So they possibly came together to the United States.

We now realize this history should have begun years ago. There is a picture of Aunt Grace (Gesia Mui) and Uncle William (Wilmoom) Wilterdink and their son Albert.

Albert married his cousin, Pa's (John Beld) youngest sister, Grace Beld in 1908. Grace died August 1, 1911. They had one child who also died at the age of eighteen. So, there is no family history from that source.

Where no questions were asked, no answers were given. Sorry about that.

Grandmother, Anje Bos-Beld, being the only living child of great grandfather and great grandmother Bos, stayed living on their (her parent's) farm after marrying Henry John Beld (our grandfather).

Anje and John Beld were married by Reverend S. Bolks at Zeeland, Michigan on December 10, 1865. The marriage was witnessed by A. Van Bree and H. Keppel.

Anje's father gave them their start in cattle, purebred Herefords, which were considered the best, or prize-winning cattle.

Life for these early settlers, like for many other pioneer settlements in America, was very plain and full of hardships.

There were no roads to speak of. Travel was largely over paths or Indian trails through the (Michigan) woods.

Church was the focal point of community life.

Father Beld was a deacon and the records found in George Beld's father's possessions are from 1883 to 1888. Also, in that book was the original birth certificate of mother, Anje Bos-Beld, dated February 26, 1847. Another birth certificate was dated December 26, 1815, which could be our great grandmother since it was written in Holland and the writing is not too plain. But, we think this is so very interesting.

Interesting also is the old family Bible with all the dates of births, marriages, and deaths which the Bible is in the possession of Jame Beld Nelson (who is the youngest daughter of John Harm Beld and Suzzanne Allaart-Beld) who are living at 3581 Eucalyptus Avenue, Riverside, California.

Copied from the old family Bible:[16]

Hendrick Jon Beld in Noort Amerika gekomen in hit jaar onzen Heere 1857. In October maant geboren 1840 in de gemente Glenkamp Graafschaap Benthim Germany Keizenyk Preusen. En myn vrourv Anje Belo-Bos in Noort Amerika gekomen in het jaar 1848. Is geboren in de gemente Leens te Gronigen, Nederland.

---

[16] Translated from Dutch to English using Google Translate: "Hendrick Jon Beld came to North America in the year of our Lord 1857. Born in October 1840 in the community of Glenkamp, County of Bentheim, Germany, Kingdom of Prussia. And my wife Anje Belo-Bos came to North America in the year 1848. She was born in the community of Leens in Groningen, Netherlands."

Great grandmother Beld died at age eighty-eight on January 28, 1893. Great grandfather Beld died at age ninety-six on November 8, 1895.

Hendrik Jan Beld of Zeeland in the state of Michigan and Anje Belo-Bos of Zeeland in the state of Michigan on December year 1865 joined together by S. Boulks, witnessed by A. Van Bree and H. Keppel. Brother, Wietze Bos, died August 19, 1871. Father Jan Bos died August 4, 1886.

Chapter 12

Beld History from Memory

(By Grace Beld-Vander Veen)

After writing down some things I thought were worth remembering, I came across a page that I copied from the old Beld Bible. In it was the date of our grandfather, Hendrick Jan Beld's mother and father's death.

So, this is our great grandmother Beld who died at age eighty-eight on January 28, 1893. Great grandfather died at age ninety-six on November 8, 1895.

The date 1893 was the year sister Jennie was born and the second date 1895 was the year sister Gertie[17] was born.

I can't remember our parents ever mentioning them, but our father's father, Hendrik Jan Beld, came to America in 1857. He was born October 23, 1840, in Graafshcaap, Bentheim, Germany. That is on the German-

[17] This Gertie was Joyce Anderson's mother.

Holland border. So, he was seventeen years of age when he came to America.

Our father's mother, Anje Belo-Bos, was born on February 26, 1847 in Groningen, the Netherlands. She came with her parents and brothers to America in 1848 having her first birthday on the sail boat.[18]

While making the trip on the sail boat, which took forty days. An epidemic of small pox broke out and some people died and were buried at sea.

One of grandmother's brothers also was buried at sea. The deaths of her one brother, Wietze Beld, also in the Bible, died August 19, 1872. Her father, Jan Bos, died August 4, 1886.

She (apparently Anje Belo-Bos) also had deaths, births, and marriages of our grandfather and her children up to the time of her death at age forty-eight. So, after that is what our mother and father had record of and what they've told me so I could record.

Anyway, our grandparents lived on the farm owned first by grandmother's parents, the Bos's. There

---

[18] Some of this information is repeated from earlier chapters. That is often the case here with 72-year-old Grace Beld-Vander Veen repeating some stories. Readers, please keep in mind, the text from which I used was originally typed on a typewriter, before computers were available and many years before Internet access allowed genealogical programs and tracking. Though some of the information is repeated, like every story, more details are revealed.

were two houses and our grandfather and grandmother lived in the big house—they had a big family.

How our grandparents met, I don't think our parents knew, or at least they never mentioned it that I can remember.

This is recorded in the family Bible: Hendrick Jan Beld of Zeeland, Michigan and Anje Belo-Bos of Zeeland, Michigan were joined together in marriage on December 10, 1865 by S. Boulks and witnessed by A. Van Bree and H. Keppel.

Grandfather, Hendrik Jan Beld, was born October 23, 1840, and died April 18, 1889. Grandmother, Anje Belo-Bos, was born February 26, 1847, and died December 1, 1895.

To the union ten children were born. The oldest, John Harm Beld was born October 23, 1867 and married Nelle De Young on February 23, 1887. She died October 6, 1887.

Their second child was a girl, Zwaantie, born November 7, 1869, and died May 13, 1870.

Next was our father, John Beld, born July 25, 1870, and died September 20, 1961. He married our mother, Gertie Heetderks who was born August 24, 1868, and died April 18, 1944.

How they met, I think we all know, but for those of you who don't know, I'll tell you it's a story you'll not forget.

Our mother was the hired girl at the Henry John Beld farm and working at a family like that never could do any harm.

You see, our mother and father's parents came from the same place in Bentheim, Germany and were second cousins of the same race.

The lady of the house (our grandmother) you understand was a seamstress, cook, and flower loving woman who could work to beat the band. So, mother didn't stand around or primp with her beautiful hair.

Mother said she seen grandma with a white cloth wiping off the stairs to see if any dirt was left after mother had mopped and cleaned.

It was always like that. She (grandmother) was a perfectionist it seemed. With those grown boys around—see there were three. The three teen girls as well kept looking sweet and dirt free. But, in spite of work and love for family, our mother stayed on.

I think she had her eyes fixed already on the next son, John. You see, John Harm was married now and our dad was next to go. Since grandmother liked our mother—sure our dad put on a good show.

They started courting and although their parents were very strict, our father untied mother's apron strings and grandmother frowned on that little trick.

Now, if that's the worst our father done, and they could admit we better just confess we've done worse and are still at it.

Now in 1887, Uncle John Harm's bride of eight months passed away. So sorrow came to visit them and times were not so gay.

Then in April of 1889 our grandfather suddenly too was called home. Grandmother was so lonely and felt so alone. So, she asked father and mother to get married and stay to help her on the farm and be with her every day.

So, they were married May 17, 1889.

Now Uncle John Harm too got married again to Susan Aallart on April 10, 1890. He was a young widower and I don't have any record of where they lived until in Grant, Michigan.

They were neighbors to our family. Our part in the Beld clan started and fell into line.

Our father's mother (our grandmother) married again to Jacob Glerum on March 25, 1891.

This disappointed her sons and daughters which sent them on the run.

Well, our parents got their start at that grand old Michigan farm and in spite of all that happened there, it still remained a clan.

It was our parents that gave the first grandchild to the clan. She is living yet. It is none other than our dear sister Ann.

Ann was born in Zeeland on September 19, 1891, and named after Grandma Beld.

They soon moved away to Wayland, Michigan—a place they hadn't beheld. From there, they moved to Grand Rapids—the furniture city in 1892.

That year, two of our father's sisters got married: Jane to Martin Van Duine on April 6, 1892; and Zwaantje, (or Cynthia as she was later called) married William Prince on October 14, 1892.

In Grand Rapids our second sister, Jennie, was born on May 5, 1893. She was named for our mother's mother to keep peace in the family tree.

The naming after fathers and mothers, then followed by brothers and sisters was very important in those good old, or bad old, days.

Our parents now had competition. Uncle John Harm's family also had a boy craze.

Our parents were blessed with another well-born baby girl. Mother suggested naming her Wilma after her father which made our father's head whirl. No Wilma would do for his new baby girl. All he could think of was boys and on he would strive.

So this new addition was named Gertie[19]. She was born June 3, 1895. I think she was named for our mother, although she had a sister Gertrude, too.

Anyway, our father got his way and mother's ideas wouldn't do.

The year 1895 was a year of mixed emotions for the Beld family.

Our father's mother gave birth to a baby girl, Marie Glerum on November 13, 1895, and just eighteen days later, on December 1, 1895, their mother passed away.

The youngest Beld children at home yet were Uncle Henry age fourteen, Aunt Anna age eleven, and Aunt Grace age eight.

Now, back to our family. Two years later the son our father wanted came and named him Henry John Beld who was born March 29, 1897.

Henry John grew to be a big strong man and served our family well until the flu came along in 1918 which took Henry to Heaven.

It seems the family decided to move again to Grant, Michigan—maybe to put the children to work so they'd be an honor to the family.

---

[19] Gertie was Joyce Anderson's mother.

At Grant, they tried to make a farm in the woods which was not too easy to do. With more relatives trying the same, it seemed logical.

Although the dampness didn't agree with mother--her health began to fail.

You see, Tuberculosis was bad and that disease sure did prevail.

Well, a sickly baby boy was born September 21, 1899. They named him William after mother's father. Two days later, this baby died which too was hard on our mother.

Now at this time another of father's brothers was to be married. It was Uncle Wietze who took Anna Hesselink January 25, 1900, to be his bride. They decided too in the woods of Grant, Michigan to reside.

Well again in our family on September 19, 1901, another boy was born and was named again for mother's father who was by now quite forlorn.

But this William too was a sickly baby with troubles galore. If you don't believe me, ask Ann. She will tell you more.

William was born on Ann's tenth birthday, so whenever he cried, Ann, being the oldest, carried him around. He just couldn't be denied. I just don't dare to say too much. You see, Willie got well and done alright.

It was a big family now and they're almost all here tonight.

Well, just two years later on August 17, 1903, another boy came along. They named him after our proud father John. You see, our father had brothers too and they named a son John. I just hope there is one her tonight to let us know the name was carried on. [20]

[20] These last two paragraphs appear out of context unless Grace Beld Vander Veen wrote this while hosting Beld siblings.

Chapter 12E

Explanation and Details

(By Gary W. Wietgrefe)

Each generation tends to look at past generation in a static environment. That is wrong. Each generation tried to progress with age. Younger adults think they know better than their parents or grandparents. Better, they set out to prove they are right. That is how change occurs.

Consider the sail boat voyage of Anje Bos-Beld to America in 1848. Sail boats had been used for over 5,000 years since Egyptians and Mesopotamians navigated the seas. Anje's family likely never questions the transportation mode.

Why didn't they take a steam or diesel powered cruise ship? Better, why didn't her family just fly the twelve hours from Amsterdam to Grand Rapids, Michigan?

In 1819 the SS Savannah crossed from Savannah, Georgia to Liverpool, England in a hybrid sail/steam ship. Obviously, that was not standard adopted technology by 1848.

The reason the Bos family didn't fly to American was that airplanes weren't invented yet. In fact, a century after the steam assisted ship sailed the Atlantic, in 1919 two guys, John Alcock and Arthur Brown, made the first transatlantic flight from St. John's Newfoundland, Canada to Clifden, Ireland.

Taking so long to make the Atlantic crossing in crowded ship conditions eating from one centralized kitchen allowed communicable diseases, like smallpox, to spread rapidly. Without refrigeration to preserve the bodies, funerals were held at sea and bodies dumped overboard—as had been done for thousands of years.

Why didn't the Beld family get vaccinated for smallpox?

If you thought there was not smallpox vaccine in 1848, you would be wrong.

Forty-seven year old Edward Jenner invented the first vaccine in 1796. It was for small pox, (now written smallpox). Jenner is considered the father of immunology. He is credited for saving more lives than any man, except Jesus.

Jenner's vaccine invention, like any technology, is of no use unless implemented. Too many times people horde their good ideas, charge for them, or are restricted by government from implementing ideas that benefited mankind.

We should thank homesteaders, like the Belds, who arrived at their grassless Holland Center homestead dirt poor by wagon. They survived many trials to produce food for themselves and others.

From oceans through the Plains, railroads distributed grains, meat, vegetables, and fruits throughout the country making everyone healthier.

Devout pioneers reared their children in faith, work and tenacity. America prospered.

The next time you have a chance, thank the few remaining grandchildren of homesteaders, like my friend and neighbor, ninety-nine year old Joyce Anderson.

While you are at it, also thank her 88-year-old baby brother, Marvin, who still works in California redeveloping malls. Of course, be sure to thank Joyce's 91-year-old brother, John.

Oh, don't forget to thank her oldest brother Severn who is 102 and lives on his California almond farm.

Chapter 13

Go West

(By Grace Beld-Vander Veen)

Now the relatives living in Grant, Michigan, during the same struggling years visited each other regularly and shared their joys and tears.

They saw our mother's health beginning to fail so fast. They all knew the doctor was right. The way she was, she would never last.

(A large family group was organized which consisted of:

1. John, his wife, Gertie, daughters Annie, Jennie, Gertie, Henry John, William, and John Jr.);
2. Our father's oldest sister, Jane (who married Martin Van Duine) and their three children; and
3. Our father's brother, Wietze (who married Anna Hessenlinkn) and their two little girls.

All decided as quick as a wink to look for another place to live. Since mother's doctor said, "Go West," they followed an ad in the newspaper about an excursion. What a jest![21]

Anyway, they really got serious and told it to Uncle William Wilterdink. He put them in contact with a land agent.

Now they were in pink!

Soon they were on their way with John Rooks as their guide to western South Dakota and looking over homesteads with joy and with pride.

I like to think our father was a popular, industrious man because three other families followed his indirect plan to venture out west.

They all had to start from scratch.

How did they dare to do it with their families attached?

Well, anyway, all three took up homesteads in that far away place. After returning still another good friend joined in to embrace.

He too decided to go. So, all together one day they held a sale.

It somehow seems ridiculous, but they were not about to fail. They kept their few pieces of furniture; beds,

---

[21] "What a jest" is an old colloquialism meaning "What a joke" usually meant to be funny. A Jester was a professional jokester or played and dress the fool in medieval courts.

wagon, and stove. Then they packed them in an emigrant box car to shove off for their cove.

The nearest railroad station, Hettinger, North Dakota, was still twenty-one miles away from their homesteads they had filed.

Since there was no telephone in those days, a letter was written to the Le Febres (John, Dick, and Fred) that the box car had been loaded and sent on ahead.

These men (Le Febres) had filed on homesteads too and were batching till they could get their houses made—then do their matching.

They were very glad to see some new people coming in. So, they would be willing to help these emigrants with all their kin.

Our parents, relatives and friends were now busy saying goodbye.

Our mother's parents were still living at Graafschap yet. They said good bye to all the relatives they were leaving behind hoping all would be remembering them in this adventure of a different kind.

They took the boat to Chicago. From there, they took a train.

Hettinger, North Dakota, July 15, 1908, was the next stop and there they would have to remain until the Le Febres came to help them unload and load.

The nearest railroad station Hettinger, North Dakota was still 21 miles away from the homesteads they had filed and no telephone in those days. So a letter was written to the leFebres (John, Dick, and Fred) that the boxcar had been loaded and sent on ahead. These men had filed on homesteads too and were batching till they could get their houses made, then do their matching. They were very glad to see some new people coming in, so would be willing to help these emigrants with all their kin. Our parents, relatives and friends were now busy saying goodbye. Our mothers' parents were still living at Graafschap yet. They said good bye to all the relatives they were leaving behind, hoping all would be remembering them in this adventure of a different kind. They took the boat to Chicago and from there took the train. Hettinger, North Dakota, July 15, 1908, was the next stop and there they would have to remain until the leFebres came to help them unload and load and can't you see them going to the homesteads without any roads. They had trouble with the tires on the wheels always coming off so they had to stop and pound them back on, it really made them cough.

Sisters Annie and Jennie had to go to Lemmon to work in a Hotel, so wasn't with the rest of the family the clan of the Belds. Anyway, they finally arrived at the place they had to homestead and put up a little shelter with boards-just a shade for their head. They had no mattresses so used the warm ground for a bed. The weather was hot and dry not much grass upon the land because the ranchers had cattle and sheep that ate it to the sand. The men all got busy making their sod houses, some called them shacks, I'm sure it was interesting to see them start from scratch. All I know is what they told me and that they had hard times. Hardly had enough to eat and later got coal from the mines. Before the time of getting coal they would burn cow chips for heat. Our mother was thrifty and could bake bread no one could beat, water was another problem they had to carry that from a creek. And that was a mile and a half away so it made them really meek. It took about nine days to build a sod house without windows, floor or door, but they kept busy at it till all had houses and more. The very first Sunday that Le Febres came and the clan all assembled together. Fred read a sermon and they sang and worshipped enjoying each other, soon after the service it started to rain, so as quick as you could say able our parents got under a umbrella and the young ones under the table. We can surely say these were years to remember and because of our mother's health they had a lot to surrender. I think those two or three room houses were so

Can't you see them going to the homesteads without any roads?

They had trouble with the tire on the wheels always coming off. So, they had to stop and pound them back on. It really made them cough.

(Photo: original page from Beld Family History.)

Sisters, Annie and Jennie, had to go to Lemmon to work in a hotel, so they weren't with the rest of the family clan of Belds.

Anyway, they finally arrived at the place they had to homestead and put up a little shelter with boards—just a shade for their head.

They had no mattresses, so used the warm ground for a bed.

The weather was hot and dry and not much grass upon the land because ranchers had cattle and sheep that ate it to the sand.

The men all got busy making their sod houses. Some called them shacks.

I'm sure it was interesting to see them start from scratch. All I know is what they told me.

They had hard times. Hardly had enough to eat and later got coal from the mines.

Before the time of getting coal, they would burn cow chips for heat.

Our mother was thrifty and could bake bread no one could beat.

Water was another problem. They had to carry water from a creek—a mile and a half away. So, it made them really meek.

It took nine days to build a sod house without windows, floor, or door. But, they kept busy at it till all had houses and more.

The very first Sunday Le Febres came and the clan all assembled together.

Fred read a sermon and they sang and worshipped enjoying each other.

Soon after the service, it started to rain. So, as quick as you could say "able," our parents got under an umbrella and young ones under the table.

We can surely say these were years to remember. Because of our mother's health, they had a lot to surrender.

I think those two or three room houses were so neat made of sod. They didn't need big houses then. They lived like peas in a pod.

Living at first without windows, doors, or roof—they waited for our father to earn money with no time to goof.

There were no fences or roads.

Everyone trying to get a start, I wonder did all those Michiganders think they were smart?...Way out there in the wild and woolly Middle West, far from relatives in Michigan—the state their forefathers loved best?

Chapter 14

Plastered

(By Grace Beld-Vander Veen)

Sisters Ann and Jennie (ages 16 and 15) had to go to Lemmon to work. So, they didn't come to the claim till later…to tell their experiences and how they didn't shirk.

Their work wasn't easy.

Working in a hotel, they never had worked out before[22]; so had they had some big, long stories to tell.

After seeing the humble little sod home and three brothers and sister, Gertie[23], who was with mother at home, the oldest two girls left again.

---

[22] "Worked out" at a hotel has certainly changed meanings. Author's context, "worked out" meant employed somewhere besides at home or farm. Now, most modern hotels imitate physical work by having exercise rooms with weights, barbells, and treadmills (an exercise device on a moving belt to walk or run in place).

[23] This was the only sentence where mother Gertie and daughter Gertie were mentioned together. Gertie, the daughter, was Joyce Anderson's mother.

It was sad to see them going thirty-five miles away. The had to earn some money to help our father pay for the things needed on the farm and get livestock to put in the barn.

Well, those years were poor. They didn't get a crop. They worked hard for nothing, but they still didn't stop.

Henry and Gertie walked miles for white sand to plaster the walls[24] to make the sod house look grand.

They carried the water a mile and a half. Now you kids have it easy—I can see you laugh.

(Photo: Sod house of Martin and Jane Van Duine, daughter Anje, and sons Anthony and Henry. Outside also plastered, called stucco.)

[24] Plaster (generally a mixture of lime, cement, sand and water) was mixed, applied to inside and outside sod walls, and let dry to give a smooth clean finish. Plasters natural gray color was generally painted white, or white-washed, to brighten the inside of the naturally dark enclosure. Wooden floors and cleanable walls likely added to the health of mother, Gertie.

Our fathers and mothers really did see hard times. It's a wonder they didn't give up instead of climb to see what the years ahead would do for them.

It was our mother's health that improved so much. That was the gem.

The dry climate, living out of doors, and in sunshine helped her to live the longest of her (Heetderks) family line.

Our parents never ceased to give God the praise for His goodness to them and lengthening mother's days.

Now, it was one year since they left Michigan. Our Aunt Anna, Uncle Wietze's wife, got terribly sick. She delivered a baby boy, but five days later God took her life.

She knew she was going to die.

She was such a sick lady, so naturally she was so concerned about their new baby. They named him Gerrit John Beld. He was born July 2, 1909.

By her bedside was Uncle Wietze, our mother and Aunt Jane Van Duine. They tried so hard to console her, but death was at the door.

She heard the angels signing and saw Jesus on the shore. So in haste, she asked over and over, "Who will take the baby?"

Aunt Jane said she would. But, she too was a sickly lady. Then our mother promised, "If Jane can't have him, then I will" and did.

This was such a sad experience. Aunt Anna's last bid was that Uncle Wietze take her and the little girls back to Michigan where she wanted to be buried. She wanted the girls to go with their mother's body.

Our father (who was working in Lemmon) had received a letter from our mother saying Aunt Anna was very sick, so come home.

While on his way, he stopped in (Hettinger) to ask the Doctor how things were at home.

The doctor told him of the death and that Uncle Wietze and the girls were coming with the body. So, our father didn't go home, but went with Uncle Wietze and the girls instead. He knew Uncle Wietze needed him so they went right ahead.

After the sad funeral, they visited the relatives and caught up on the news.

Our father's youngest sister, Grace, married Albert Wilterdink in November 1908. They had a baby girl named Grace.

I just had to relate.

You see, I'm named after them.

I think I forgot to name our father's sister Anna, too. She married Gerrit Mellema on July 17, 1906.

Now, after reading their red letter date[25], I even forgot our father's youngest brother, Henry, who married Addellia Gress on June 6, 1900.

These three went to live with the Wilterdinks when their mother passed away. So our father didn't have them in his story that he wrote one day.

You see, the information that I have is really all old news, but I thought you all should know it. I have no other excuse.

Well, anyway, getting back to our father and Uncle Wietze—they came back to South Dakota and worked with a threshing crew which took them to Montana and North Dakota.

While in Montana, Uncle Wietze met Lucy Weidenaar. They struck up a friendship that did not go ajar.

Now, while mother had Uncle Wietze's baby, she was experiencing another test. The baby, Gerrit John, got pneumonia and our mother couldn't rest. Gerrit became so terribly sick they thought he was going to die.

The pneumonia finally settled on his leg and made everyone cry.

---

[25] "Red letter date" apparently refers to correspondence received by Beld family author, Grace Beld-Vander Veen.

The doctor wrote, when it was ripe, he'd come and lance the leg. So, that is just what happened. Mother didn't have to beg.

The doctor came with horse and buggy and really fixed him up. As the leg healed, it stayed shorter than the other; so, Gerritt always crippled badly, but he always loved our mother.

[Photo circa 1910(?): Baby Garrit Beld, oldest son of Wietze and Anna Beld, at the house where he was born. It later became the first church at Holland Center.]

Chapter 14E

Explanation and Details

(By Gary W. Wietgrefe)

Each generation, especially those under thirty-years-old, think they live in the most sophisticated time. Communication only reached its zenith by education and smarts of each generation.

Facts, and a bit of historical knowledge, expose ignorance by the phase-out of abilities once considered a matter of life and death.

Author, Grace Beld-Vander Veen, grew up in a sod house in very remote northwestern South Dakota. She related a medical story and how a remote doctor, living in another state, treated a child with life-threatening pneumonia.

Beld's farmstead was only about a half mile from Holland Center. Currently, Holland Center, South Dakota is not a town—just a church. The nearest town, Lodgepole, has a population of forty-two. No doctor—never had one. Twenty-one miles away from the Beld homestead is the next largest town, population 1,074, is Hettinger, North Dakota. By 1909 it had a doctor.

Grace Beld explained how remote medical care was administered.

"Tele-medicine" is not a 21st-century invention.

Before telephones, small town prairie doctors were notified and responded by letter. Most towns, even small villages, had post offices with mail picked up and delivered daily or every-other-day to surrounding towns and railheads that carried mail.

The 1873 Postal Laws and Regulations book, Section 92, required mail delivery "as frequently as the public convenience may require."

Penny post cards were the most common communications. A short note, similar to a telegraph message, was written on one side of the standardized postcard (5 ½ x 3 ½ inches). On the other side was the sender's address, the mail-to address, and a one-cent postage stamp was affixed.

In the late 1800s, Aberdeen, SD had mail delivery twice per day within the city limits. That service ended in 1950 due to U.S. postal policies and budget constraints.

Once post cards were introduced, doctor traveled by horse and buggy phased out.

Rural electrification and rural telephone service developed simultaneously under the U.S. Department of Agriculture following passage of the Rural Electrification

Act of 1936 and subsequent addition of rural telephone service.

On a personal note, my father and mother married in 1951 and moved to a 18 x 20 feet tarpaper shack a half mile north of my grandparents farm. A singular telephone line of heavy-gauge wire had been strung the half mile between our two farmsteads on posts about ten foot tall.

Horses and cattle were kept at my grandparents place where my father used a bobsled in winter to feed cattle.

During snowstorms and blizzards, when snow prevented travel by our only vehicle, a Ford pickup truck, father would follow the telephone line which drooped to five feet between posts. In order to not get lost in blinding snow, he held our telephone line in his chopper mitts which guided his walk between the two farms to do chores twice per day.

Our old telephone line was last used in April 1959 when we abandon our old farmstead—we called it "the Little Place." It's the one I called home. Being the oldest of six boys, I would ride with my dad harvesting grain and fodder. We would have to raise the telephone line up to get a bundle rack under the lines. When our north farmstead was no longer used, our father cut the line and rolled up the wire. Eventually he removed the telephone posts and used them for fenceposts.

Farms and ranches had telephones (generally after WWII) to connect with doctors. Being there were a dozen or more farmsteads on a "party line" (several farms on one phone line), neighbors spread gossip about neighbors' health, deaths, births, indiscretions, and the like faster than the family got together to learn the news at meals.

After broadcast television became available in the 1950s, "tele-medicine" with video conferencing was initiated by the University of Nebraska in the mid-1950s.

The first time I was involved in a tele-video conference was in November 2016 when my mother and her cancer doctor had an experimental medication results consultation in Aberdeen with a specialist doctor in Sioux Falls (two hundred miles away).

As mentioned previously, labor in rural America has always been in short supply. Access to professionals was far more limited.

In the absence of professionals, literacy was important.

Educational books (like Twelve Courses in Agriculture) on farm living were produced which gave instructions on seed selection, planting and harvest timing, how to can vegetables and fruits, how to care for sick animals and people, cooking recipes and other useful tidbits.

(Photo: Twelve Courses in Agriculture, H.L Balwin Publishing Company, Better Farming Association, copyright 1915 and 1920, 1247 pages.)

Reading, even writing on postcards, phased out as improved roads allowed quicker vehicle travel for medical treatments.

Voice-to-voice, email, texting, and social media gradually replaced writing and reading books and newspapers—deemed necessary in the homesteading era.

Sadly, today even teachers not only allow, but encourage students, to listen to audio books and get rewarded for "reading books" solely by listening—not reading.

Using pencil and ink started phasing out with the typewriter (1808>) and telegraph (1840>). Writing's demise quickened with the introduction of telephone (1876>). The alternative to writing a paper letter to someone for information and entertainment began quickly phasing out with radio (1906>) and television (1928>).

Manual typewriters, replaced by electric keyboards have been replaced by audio dictation. Each technology has gradually deteriorated society's ability to read and write.

By the time I became an adult, people would joke, "The doctor's handwriting is so poor I can't read it. I hope the pharmacist can." To my knowledge, to provide clarity and accuracy, doctors no longer write paper prescriptions.

Handwriting in cursive (connected letters) has been dropped in schools. Recent graduates can't read it.

Example: My wife recently stopped into a store with her hand-written note of what she was looking for. The clerk, in her late twenties, looked at the slip of paper and said, “I’m not good at cursive.” My wife had to read the note to the employee.

Television is entertainment for older adults rather than writing to friends and relatives. Computer “screen-time” (automated electronic communication) further depleted society’s ability to write with pencil or pen.

Gerret John Beld survived pneumonia in 1909 because Gerdi Heetderks-Beld and her doctor had ability to read and write. Without electronic communication, could an SOS emergency be communicated today?

Chapter 15

Lemmon Winter

(By Grace Beld-Vander Veen)

I heard them say time and again in 1911 not even a potato was brought to the bin. No hay for the few cows to keep in the barn. A cold winter ahead, it looked bad on the farm.

That winter in February a baby was to be born, so dad made arrangements for the family to come to Lemmon where he was working.

All that could be gotten for the money they had was a little wooden shack a mile from Lemmon. But, they were glad to be nearer a doctor and have the family together again.

Can you imagine the anxiety that our mother was in?

Well, she was a sincere Christian and put her trust in the Lord, read God's word faithfully, and kept all in accord.

That cold twenty-eight degree below zero night in February, mother knew she had to have a doctor and couldn't tarry.

So, Ann's boyfriend who was there was the one sent to town to get dad and the doctor—and don't fool around. The boyfriend was Milton Olson. He even left his coat to cover mother in bed. That weather was no joke.

Well anyway, dad and the doctor walked that miserable mile and delivered that darling baby in the grandest of style.

Well, I am that baby.

I'm sure you couldn't guess why the Lord sent me to that home already suffering so much stress.

I hope you'll understand—I have to tell you this: there was quite a disappointment when mother told my oldest sis that they were going to have another baby.

Mother, being forty-three, was really needing help instead of sputtering from Annie, Jennie, and Gertie. Well anyway, they had quite a time to get used to having me around.

I had to have a glass bottle and Ann dropped that only one on the ground. So, Gertie walked to town to get another.

Oh, I sure caused some fun.

It seems that is my business—to be the troublesome one.

After the winter was over, back to the homestead we go. They loaded the wagon with all their things and foodstuff down below.

Our mother, baby Gracie, and little Gerrit and our father were on the seat. Gertie and Jack (or Johnnie as he then was called) used their feet.

Brothers, Henry (age 14) and Willie (age 12?) had left driving the cattle on ahead. So they left fairly early to be able to be at the homestead to go to bed.

One cow was tied to the wagon and was led so they could stop to milk. The bottle fed the baby that wasn't lying in a bed of silk.

On the way, the cattle got mixed with the cattle out to graze so the boys left notes on stones to tell of their troublesome ways. They did get back to their way again which was only a trail.

The trail was the one used by the government to deliver the U.S. Mail.

The Lubbers knew that the Belds were coming, so they could have a lunch ready before the journey ending.

Neighbors living miles away were very precious in those days. After being refreshed, fed, enlightened with the news, and the last graze, they went merrily on their last ten miles of their journey. They were glad when they got back to the little sod house on the prairie.

(Photo: Sod house of John and Gertie Beld. This must have been taken in spring as John is riding a two-row corn planter. Very likely this photo was taken after 1912 because before then they had no money to build an entry to their sod house.)

The next Sunday, all got together again and had church in Uncle Wietze' vacant house.

Now, Uncle Martin Van Duine was working farther west for Frank Van Slooten and he mentioned church to Le Febres, Libbers, Van Wyks, and the Beld clan. That conversation was overheard by a bachelor, Henry Kok, who went and told the Stuit brothers. The following Sunday they all came brave and bold.

Happy to see new Dutch people, it made everyone glad to meet new friends and have a place to worship which they hadn't had.

(Photo: Those named in this picture are (L-R): Fred Schwindle, cousin Henry Van Duine, Walter Dahl, brother Henry Beld, cousin Anthony Van Duine, William Schwindle, brothers John and William Beld, Aunt Jane Van Duine, Helen Dahl, teachers Mr. and Mrs. Fracker, cousins Anje Van Duine, Lillian Larson, Mrs. Schwindle, sister Gertie Beld, sister Jennie Beld, mother (Gertie-Heetderks-Beld), cousin Gerrit Beld, and Mrs. Dahl. Also, notice the grass (sod?) over the roof boards which provided insulation and protection against hail.)

It was soon decided to put a partition and benches in Uncle Wietze's sod house where they could worship quietly—occasionally visited by a mouse!

This place was later named Holland Center because of its central location.

To close the year of 1912, word came by mail that on December 23 Uncle Wietze Belda and Lucy Weidenaar would be married. So now all our father's brothers and sisters are happily married, except half-sister, Marie Glerum, who was just seventeen in 1912. So, according to the records, she tarried until 1920.

Now, I'm closing this long chapter of the Beld history to begin it again for the next reunion in 1983.

Chapter 16

Filling in Family Happenings

(By Grace Beld-Vander Veen)

Since starting this Beld story, I haven't heard from anyone who is willing to go on from where I left off. I waited long enough, or as long as I dared.

Now, to finish this is what must be done, or we will all be out of the story. So, I'll go on with another chapter as best I can.

There was a death of Aunt Grace Beld-Wilterdink on August 1, 1911. That I did not mention, nor do I remember hearing my parents say that they went for the funeral.

I know Aunt Grace was not well as she had tuberculosis and gave birth to cousin Grace who was afflicted with that and died at the age of seventeen.

Uncle Albert married again and there is no date given. We called her Aunt Mary (her maiden name I have forgotten). She did make a good stepmother for cousin Grace. That I did hear say.

My parents were too poor to travel, so I doubt that they went for the funeral.

The next funeral was of my mother's brother. January 17, 1912. I'm sure they didn't go for that funeral either as that was just before I was going to be born.

My two sisters were working and mail didn't come and go wither like today. And, being wintertime, my father had made arrangements for our family to move to the outskirts of Lemmon, South Dakota so we could be near to a doctor.

This brother, Uncle William, too had tuberculosis and looked poorly although he was teaching school at Englewood, Chicago, Illinois. He was not married.

Now, the following funeral of another of my mother's family, Aunt Jennie, died March 4, 1916. She too had tuberculosis and was single. Neither did my parents go for that funeral—I don't think.

Then a month later, April 30, 1916, my grandfather Heetderks died. Then my parents went and visited all the relatives on both sides.

My sister, Gertie, (age 21) was home to take care of me and the other sisters were married. Ann was married in 1914 and Jennie in 1915. Before, the girls worked in Lemmon. (See other chapters.)

My parents of course looked up all the relatives and came home with all the news which I don't remember them telling. There is no one left to tell me what it was.

I know that my grandmother Heetderks went to live by her youngest son, Gerrit Heetderks, until she became senile and went to Cutlerville, where she died in 1920.

For those two funerals I think my parents went after receiving telegrams of their deaths.

Now, in the meantime, Uncle John Harm Beld, the first son of our grandparents, move from Newago, Michigan to Kentucky. He worked in a cement plant there. He also worked in a cement plant in Newago, so possibly was sent there by promotion.

Anyway, in 1917 they decided to come to Dakota and lived a few miles from our parents and another sister, the Van Duines.

In Dakota, he mined coal (lignite). From Dakota they moved to Riverside, California. Three of Uncle John Harm's boys married Kentucky girls and stayed in Kentucky.

Later, the two boys did come to visit, so we did meet them with some of their children. These families still stayed in Kentucky to live—where they are today, with the exception of one daughter who lives in Novato, California.

She does not hear from other relatives either. We have both tried to contact them for more of their story, but it didn't happen.

We do know about the family of Will Beld who married Cinda Jane Sherrill. They have six children.

Henry Beld married Nanny Pack. They have four children—two boys and two girls.

James Beld married Anna Pearl Hawkins. They have five children. We have no record nor can we seem to get through to them. The letters didn't come back, but we never got an answer.

A cousin, Virgil Beld, on their way from Michigan to Florida seen in a newspaper a car accident reported of Belds. So I sent the report to the daughter who lives in Navato to see if she had heard about the accident, but she had not.

I sent money to the address given for flowers thinking that I would surely hear, but still no word came back. There is no more to write about their life in Kentucky.

The other children of Uncle John Harm lived in Dakota and later all moved to Riverside, California where the grandchildren still are living. The youngest daughter of Uncle John Harm lives in the same house where we copied the births, deaths, and marriage dates from the old Beld Bible.

Chapter 17

John Harms and Susan Beld

(By Grace Beld-Vander Veen)

Uncle John Harms and Aunt Susan's children are:

- Will Beld born June 5, 1889, died September 4, 1948.
- Susie Beld Robinson-Vlien born August 22, 1890, died July 7, 1964.
- Henry Beld born February 9, 1892, died ???
- James Beld born March 19, 1895, died ???
- Anje Beld-Norton born May 1, 1897, died September 27, 1967.
- Abraham Beld born June 6, 1899, died March 8, 1907.
- John Beld born July 14, 1901, died May 18, 1977.
- Wietze Beld born September 27, 1903, died October 27, 1932.
- Jane Beld-Nelson born January 12, 1908.

Aunt Jane Van Duine was the fourth child in our grandparents family under our father.

They moved to Dakota from Michigan with our parents and Uncle Wietze family. So they experience the same hardships as our parents did, although they moved to Kentucky in 1911 for a few years, then they came back to Dakota and stayed until the late 1920s.

Aunt Jane died September 30, 1922, from tuberculosis and not long afterward a grandchild, Cleo Axtell, died January 8, 1922.

Then, Anje, the oldest daughter (mother of Clo and Clyde Axtell) died June 11, 1924, from tuberculosis. Anje was a widow. Her husband died in 1921.

So, these were sad experiences in their families.

Chapter 18

Martin and Jane Van Duine

(By Grace Beld-Vander Veen)

Uncle Martin sold his place in Dakota to my brother, Jack, and moved back to Michigan where the family settled down to live.

Uncle Martin Van Duine died in Michigan September 4, 1933. Their family, all but one daughter the youngest, is the only one living.

The wives of Anthony and Henry, as well as the husbands of Elizabeth and Cynthia live in Grand Rapids, as do their children.

The only son of Anje (and Clyde Axtell) was raised by his grandparents, the Axtells in Lemmon, South Dakota. He now lives in Reno, Nevada.

Uncle Martin and Aunt Jane Van Duine's children are:

- Anthony Van Duine born February 25, 1893, died October 15, 1975.

- Anje Van Duine born November 24, 1896, died June 11, 1924.
- Henry John Van Duine born January 21, 1899, died April 24, 1968.
- Elizabeth Van Duine-Ritsema-Essing born September 19, 1911, died November 28, 1978.
- Cynthia Van Duine-Miller-Einig born January 20, 1914, died December 9, 1964.
- Marain Van Duine-Walthorn born September 8, 1916.

Chapter 19

Cynthia (and William) Prince

(By Grace Beld-Vander Veen)

Aunt Cynthia-Prince was the fifth child in our grandparent's family (Henry John and Anjie Bos-Beld) and lived in Michigan all of her married life. Her husband, or our uncle William worked for some railroad company as well as I can remember hearing our parents mentioning. They always lived in Holland, Michigan. Their Children are:

- Nick Prince born March 14, 1893.
- Anna Prince-Cander Baan born August 26, 1896, died October 11, 1958.
- Alice Ella Prince-Boeve born June 26, 1899, died March 21, 1924.
- Henrietta Prince-Heetdeerks born May 31, 1903.
- John Henry Prince born June 12, 1906.
- Infant twins stillborn May 7, 1909—May 7, 1909.
- Wilbert Prince born May 7, 1911.
- Raymond Prince born January 17, 1915.

Chapter 20

Wietze and Anna Beld

(By Grace Beld-Vander Veen)

The sixth child of our grandparent's family (Henry John and Anjie Bos-Beld) was Uncle Wietze. I have already in the first part of this history mentioned quite a bit of Uncle Wietze's experiences as they came to Dakota with our parents. That is where Aunt Anna, Uncle Wietze's wife died July 7, 1909, only five days after their little son Gerrit's birth

Uncle Wietze took Aunt Anna's body and the two little girls, Mary and Anna, to Michigan where the funeral was held. The girls were left to live with their grandparents, the Hessilinks.

Our father went with him for the burial of Aunt Anna. Gerrit, the baby, stayed at the Van Duines. A few weeks later, our mother took him as she promised to do it if Aunt Jane couldn't keep him.

Garrit lived with us until Uncle Wietze married again and settled in Montana.

I don't remember just when they came back to Dakota, but I think it must have been when Elke was a baby—so early in the 1920s.

They lived near our parents on the homestead he (Wietze) filed on. Their son, Henry, lives there yet today.

Their sod house, while vacant, served as the Holland Center Church until the frame church was built.

Before that, the three families (Belds) took turns having church in their sod houses each Sunday.

I know our sewing machine, with its box over the machine, was the pulpit. The men took turns reading the sermon.

In those days, there was no pastor.

The first pastor, Reverend John Rubingh, came in 1927.

The services, as well as Catechism, were all in the Holland language.

Those Sundays were wonderful to look forward to, even if we very seldom had even classical appointment.

The children of Uncle Wietze and Aunt Anna are:

- Gerrit Beld born October 1900, died November 1900.
- Mary Beld-Brink born July 28, 1902, died May 12, 1976.

- Anna Beld-Postma born July 2, 1904, died March 1984.
- Gertrude Beld born June 1905, died August 1905.
- Cynthia Beld born June 1906, died August 1906.
- Gerrit Beld born July 2, 1909, died June 24, 1974.

The children of Uncle Wietze and Aunt Lucy are:

- John Wietze Beld born October 28, 1913.
- Jane Janet Beld born July 9, 1915.
- Henry John Beld born May 23, 1917.
- Elke John Beld born September 3, 1919, died August 7, 1954.
- John Harm Beld born October 23, 1922.
- Bertha Anna Beld born December 9, 1925.

Aunt Lucy died April 10, 1939. Uncle Wietze died November 20, 1948.

Chapter 21

Anje Beld

(By Grace Beld-Vander Veen)

The seventh child of our grandparents (Henry John and Anjie Bos-Beld) only lived seven months. They named her Anje Beld. She was born March 13, 1880, and died October 29, 1880.

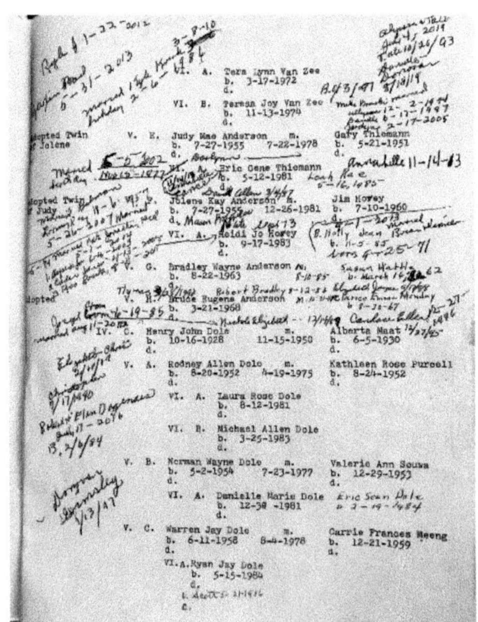

VI. A. Tera Lynn Van Zee
b. 3-17-1972
d.

VI. B. Teresa Joy Van Zee
b. 11-13-1974
d.

Adopted Twin of Jolene — V. E. Judy Mae Anderson m. 7-22-1978 Gary Thiemann
b. 7-27-1955 — b. 5-21-1951
d. — d.

VI. A. Eric Gene Thiemann
b. 5-12-1981
d.

Adopted Twin of Judy — V. F. Jolene Kay Anderson m. 12-26-1981 Jim Hovey
b. 7-27-1955 — b. 7-10-1960
d. — d.

VI. A. Heidi Jo Hovey
b. 9-17-1983
d.

V. G. Bradley Wayne Anderson
b. 8-22-1963
d.

Adopted — V. H. Bruce Eugene Anderson
b. 3-21-1968
d.

IV. C. Henry John Dole m. 11-15-1950 Alberta Maat
b. 10-16-1928 — b. 6-5-1930
d. — d.

V. A. Rodney Allen Dole m. 4-19-1975 Kathleen Rose Purcell
b. 8-20-1952 — b. 8-24-1952
d. — d.

VI. A. Laura Rose Dole
b. 8-12-1981
d.

VI. B. Michael Allen Dole
b. 3-25-1983
d.

V. B. Norman Wayne Dole m. 7-23-1977 Valerie Ann Souwa
b. 5-2-1954 — b. 12-29-1953
d. — d.

VI. A. Danielle Marie Dole
b. 12-30-1981
d.

V. C. Warren Jay Dole m. 8-4-1978 Carrie Frances Meeng
b. 6-11-1958 — b. 12-21-1959
d. — d.

VI. A. Ryan Jay Dole
b. 5-15-1984
d.

(Photo: Example of back pages Beld Family history book.)

Chapter 22

Henry John Beld and Addillia Gress-Beld

(By Grace Beld-Vander Veen)

The eight child of our grandparents (Henry John and Anjie Bos-Beld) was Henry John Beld. He was born September 6, 1881.

Soon after the death of his mother in 1895, he and his sisters, Anna and Grace, went to live with their father's sister, Mrs. William Wilterdink and her husband in rural Holland, Michigan.

He lived with them until his marriage in May 1900 to Addillia Gress of Grand Rapids, Michigan. She had immigrated from Canada in 1895.

At the time of Henry John's marriage in Grand Rapids, he took employment as a delivery man with the Blake bakery. That bakery distributed baked goods to grocery stores.

Later, he was employed as a metal polisher and buffer at the Keeler Brass Company and the Wolverine Brass Works.

Their first home was on Knapp Road in north Grand Rapids. They soon moved to B Street near the Grace Reformed Church which was to be their home church all of their lives.

At this residence, their first child, George, was born January 7, 1903.

They then moved farther south to Godfrey Avenue where their second son, Cameron, was born.

A few years later, they moved to Fifth Avenue (now Franklin Street) where their third son, Donald, was born February 18, 1908.

In the spring of 1908 they decided to try "muck farming" by raising onions and celery in Decatur, Michigan.

While living in Decatur, their fourth son, Gerald, was born August 21, 1909.

In 1910, they returned to Grand Rapids and lived on Crofton Street.

Upon their return to Grand Rapids, Henry decided to attend the Michigan College of Chiropractic in Grand Rapids. There he studied and graduated becoming a practicing Doctor of Chiropractic.

He did chiropractic full time until 1912 when he gave up full time practice to take employment at his old trade polishing and buffing refrigerator hardware at the Leonard Refrigerator Company. That company later merged and formed the Kelvinator Corporation.

Henry continued working at Kelvinator until the time of his death in 1952.

From Crofton Street in 1911, the family moved to Roosevelt Avenue.

In 1912 their fifth child, and only daughter, Esther, was born March 24, 1912.

In 1914, they purchased their own home was to serve as their residence until their death.

It was here their sixth child, Virgil, was born on March 10, 1916.

Henry served as a deacon and elder in the Grace Reformed Church from 1908 until the time of his death. He was active in Sunday School.

He also served thirty-one years as a member of Godfrey Lee School Board for over twenty-five years as president of the board.

Henry was also active in several other religious and civic organizations.

Henry and Addillia's children are:

- George Henry Beld born January 7 1903; died February 21, 1979.

- Cameron Garner Beld born July 12, 1904, died July 6, 1968.
- Donald Oliver Beld born February 18, 1908, died December 7, 1969.
- Gerald Franklin Beld born August 21, 1909, died March 8, 1966.
- Esther Grace Beld born March 24, 1912.
- Virgil Burdette Beld born March 10, 1916.

Uncle Henry passed away August 2, 1952, after about a year's illness. Death was due to abdominal cancer.

Uncle Henry's wife, Aunt Addillia, survived him and died from a coronary thrombosis May 11, 1955.

Chapter 23

Anje Anna Beld-Mellema and Gerrit Mellema

(By Grace Beld-Vander Veen)

The ninth child of our grandparents (Henry John and Anjie Bos-Beld) as born June 3, 1884 in Beaverdam, Michigan and lived with their father's sister, Mrs. William Wilterdink and her husband in rural Holland, Michigan until her marriage to Gerrit Mellema. He was a grocer who owned his own store at 101 Franklin Street in Grand Rapids.

They purchased their first home close to the store. After the birth of their first child, a larger home was purchased at 930 Shelden Avenue.

The Mellemas were among the first members of the First Christian Reformed Church of Grand Rapids. All their children were baptized here. Later, all made their Public Profession of Faith here.

Their children are:

- Elizabeth Mellema-Hiemstra born February 6, 1908.
- Angeline Mellema born March 3, 1909, died March 30, 1912.
- Henry Mellema born July 19, 1910.
- Angeline Mellema born November 6, 1912, died November 26, 1920.
- Grace Mellema-De Groot born November 21, 1914.
- Robert Mellema born October 3, 1918.
- William Mellema born September 8, 1920.

Aunt Anna Mellema suffered a stroke in May 1945 which left her partially paralyzed until her death June 27, 1959. Uncle Gerrit died August 27, 1964.

Chapter 24

Gesien Miena Beld

(By Grace Beld-Vander Veen)

The tenth child (the last of this union) was baptized and named Gesien Miena Beld. That is according to our grandmother's own handwriting and written in the old family Bible. She was called Grace by the brothers and sisters.

Aunt Grace, born June 22, 1887, also lived with their father's sister Mrs. William Wilterdink and her husband in rural Holland, Michigan until her marriage to her cousin Albert Wilterdink.

They only had one child, Grace Wilterdink who was born in 1909.

Aunt Grace died August 1, 1911, so their baby lived with the grandparents until Uncle Albert remarried to Mary (?). The child Grace died at the age of seventeen on July 31, 1928.

Uncle Albert died June 4, 1945.

Chapter 25

Marie Glerum

(By Grace Beld-Vander Veen)

The eleventh child born to our grandmother was after her marriage to Jacob Glerum. She was named Marie Glerum born November 13, 1895.

Her mother, our grandmother, only lived seventeen days after Marie's birth.

(Photo: Grandmother Anje Bos-Beld and daughters Cynthia, Grandmother, Jane, Grace, and Anna circa 1890-91.)

Marie was raised by relatives on the Glerum side.

She married Charles Rosema on May 19, 1920. They only had one son, Norman, born October 26, 1931.

Aunt Marie died December 14, 1962. Her husband Charles Rosema died June 1, 1961.

Chapter 26

Homesteader Results

(Gary W. Wietgrefe interviewed Joyce Anderson.)

November 18, 2025: "Marvin, my youngest brother, drove here from Modesto, California. Too bad you didn't get to meet him. He couldn't stay long—had to get back.

"He's a businessman—buys and refurbishes old malls," Joyce continued.

"He went to college and needed fifty dollars to take a college test. He paid for college on his own, but didn't have fifty dollars to take that test and had to work for it."

Here is where Joyce mentioned something about Marvin working on or owning a peach, almond and dairy farm. I didn't get details.

"Brother, Severn, is two and a half years older than me. January seventh he will be a hundred and two. He lives on his own almond farm about fourteen miles from Modesto, near Ripon, California.

"All my brothers and sisters moved to California. I'd move there, too, but I was married.

"My two sisters are gone. Youngest died in 2014—had cancer of the mouth.

"Anna Jean, my other sister had Crohn's disease.

"Both our parents died of cancer in Modesto, California.

"Father had a fourteen pound tumor removed and got another tumor so big that they had to hold it (the regrowth) when they moved him. He died in 1962—sixty-seven years old.

"Mom lived fourteen more years.

"My husband, George, had surgery in Rochester, Minnesota in 1996. We were still on the farm. He lived fourteen more years after heart trouble.

"George had a bleeding problem—had Factor 8. Did surgery on Thursday and three days later because I read and article of top U.S. doctor in Good Housekeeping (magazine). We got that best doctor to do surgery.

"We moved here (Rapid City) in 2005. George didn't want to move. George got Alzheimer's. Our son, Brad, moved him to Billings—Brad paid his bills. There they put him on Seroquel, so I brought him--moved him back. He died in 2008.

"I'm going blind—have Fuchs Dystrophy in my eyes. Had an implant when we were on the farm.

"George was in a quartet. Sang for fifty funerals. Those guys came to see him. After two and a half hours he couldn't remember they came. Alzheimer's.

"Holland Center Church now gets a minister from another congregation from Prairie Center, Wesleyan Methodist. He comes to preach at eight at Holland Center—been minister there for fifteen years.

"Duck Creek Lutheran Church is where we went. Had another Lutheran Church in Hettinger. That is where I went to high school. No minister in Hettinger. A nursing home nurse holds services in that big Lutheran church in Hettinger. Covid did a bad thing for churches.[26]

"Young people come to our church. No school so they home school their children. Those young people work for ranchers."

They live a long ways from school. Does Lodgepole have a school?

"Brad went to Duck Creek one-room school for eight years. Our sons, Bruce and Brad were valedictorians in Hettinger High School. They were good in music. All our girls played piano.

---

[26] Belds left The Netherlands 147 years earlier, 1857, because all churches were federally operated. Preaching was regulated. They could not minister to groups over twenty in order to control the many religious protests against government control. During the Covid epidemic (2020-21) governments around the world, including the U.S., banned gatherings, including group worship.

"Bruce learned the pipe organ. They live in St. Paul (Minnesota). He gave a concert to twenty-four organists around the Minneapolis/St. Paul area.

"Lodgepole had a grocery store, post office and an appliance store. It still sells appliances in Lodgepole. Susan, Brad's wife, probably bought her new appliance there.

"They kept the four-room house and tore the entryway off and remodeled it. They will retire at our farm.

"They got married in 1985. Spent a year in Germany after Oral Roberts graduation. Susan's dad was an Air Force pilot. He went down in water, crashed, when she was three. Her mother remarried.

"Brad and Susan are redoing the farmhouse. Brad only wants to have sheep. It's fenced for sheep. John Green runs sheep on the farm.

"In 2005, Brad bought our farm including the Helen Knutson place."

Joyce mentioned a few things of each of her children. She was so proud she adopted each of them and of course had Brad. She told me what each of them did, where they lived, and how she gets to talk to them on the phone when they can't come to see her.

Joyce is going blind. She's obviously legally blind. I had been working with the South Dakota State Library on their "Talking Books" program. A program to record books on audio and make them available free of charge to visually impaired South Dakotans.

I had the State Library computer, microphone and a 9:00 A.M. appointment to record Joyce's memories. About 8:30 she called me.

"I can't do the recording. I can't have my voice recorded. There are scammers out there. I got scammed bad on the phone and I can't let them get my voice. I trust you but I can't afford to be scammed again."

I was so interested in Joyce and her homesteading family. What a fascinating story from a ninety-nine year old lady—the daughter of homesteaders.

I responded, "Joyce we don't have to do a recording. Can I just come and visit with you and take notes?"

"Oh, that will be ok."

I kept the appointment. It became one of the most fascinating conversations I have ever had. Joyce is so sincere. She wanted other people to know how tough she had it, but worse how hard it was for her grandpa and grandma, mother, father, aunts and uncles and others that came from Michigan to homestead some of the last available ground. Bare, utterly grassless South Dakota prairie in the summer of 1908 grew thriving families by 2025.

We gradually finished the long conversation as her interim care person, Fay Hanson, who comes in for an hour, was about to arrive.

"She drives from Hermosa. We get along good. She was originally from Minnesota and only had enough money to get to Rapid City," Joyce was happy to report.

I had been sitting on Joyce's living room couch. She was in her comfortable chair facing her large picture window with sun reflecting her front yard. To my right, was another chair she uses. Its back to the bright window. Beside that chair was a side-table with a stack, maybe an inch thick, of large (4"x6"?) recipe cards with large writing.

Sometimes in the morning when I would stop to visit Joyce, she was sitting with her back to the eastern window. Sun would flood her living room. It was there, with her limited sight, she could still read some things in her dimming blindness.

"What are those cards on your end table?" I asked.

At ninety-nine, Joyce explained. "My sight is not good enough to read the Bible, which I wanted to read again beginning to end. Instead, I wrote down passages large enough I can still read and memorize them. I have many more on my desk.

"I used to have Bible study at my place."

A couple months earlier, my wife and I were in town one of the days of her monthly Bible study. We attended with a neighbor, DW and Pam Leaman. DW led the small group.

Joyce went on, "We sometimes had twelve around the dining table for Bible study. That's a new table."

I glanced into the dining room.

"One lady said she was going to stop attending because there was no more room at the table. So I bought a bigger table."

I looked around, then down at my many pages of notes and realized Joyce's stories had an underlying narrative, allegory—hidden meaning.

The last generation of homesteaders, religiously persecuted in their home country, found a baren refuge in what many called a "God-forsaken" land.

Her mother's one-room sod house was built in nine days. The Third Commandment, "Remember the Sabbath day and keep it holy," was not ignored because there was no roof—no building.

Families and neighbors, who helped each other built the crudest structures, gathered that Sunday to join in reverent celebration praising God for his gifts.

A hundred and seventeen years had passed since those last homesteaders and their children sat on Dakota prairie grass and worshipped God.

I looked at Joyce and recalled Proverbs 22:6. "Start children off on the way they should go, and even when they are old they will not turn from it."[27]

---

[27] Holy Bible, New International Version.

As we were saying goodbyes, reminiscing of old times, Joyce said, "I can't believe I live in a place this nice. I never dreamed of living like this.

"I just keep living here on my own."

May Joyce realize how much joy she brought to her seven adopted children, her son, all their children and grandchildren, congregations, and still to her neighbors.

All are surrounded by spiritual guides, like Joyce living nearby, giving directions. May we continually learn from them and support them.

I smiled as I closed Joyce's door.

Appendix I

United States National Archives Summary of Homestead Act of 1862

Citation: Act of May 20, 1862 (Homestead Act), Public Law 37-64 (12 STAT 392); 5/20/1862; Enrolled Acts and Resolutions of Congress, 1789 - 2011; General Records of the United States Government, Record Group 11; National Archives Building, Washington, DC.

Reference link: https://www.archives.gov/milestone-documents/homestead-act.

Passed on May 20, 1862, the Homestead Act accelerated the settlement of the western territory by granting adult heads of families 160 acres of surveyed public land for a minimal filing fee and five years of continuous residence on that land.

The Homestead Act, enacted during the Civil War in 1862, provided that any adult citizen, or intended citizen, who had never borne arms against the U.S. government could claim 160 acres of surveyed government land. Claimants were required to live on and "improve" their plot by cultivating the land. After five years on the land, the original filer was entitled to the property, free and clear, except for a small registration fee. Title could also be acquired after only a six-month residency and trivial improvements, provided the claimant paid the government $1.25 per acre. After the Civil War, Union soldiers could deduct the time they had served from the residency requirements.

Although this act was included in the Republican party platform of 1860, support for the idea began decades earlier. Even under the Articles of Confederation, before 1787, the distribution of government lands generated much interest and discussion.

The act, however, proved to be no panacea for poverty. Comparatively few laborers and farmers could afford to build a farm or acquire the necessary tools, seed, and livestock. In the end, most of those who purchased land under the act came from areas quite close to their new homesteads (Iowans moved to Nebraska, Minnesotans to South Dakota, and so on). Unfortunately, the act was framed so ambiguously that it seemed to invite fraud, and early modifications by Congress only compounded the problem. Most of the land went to speculators, cattle owners, miners, loggers, and railroads. Of some 500 million acres dispersed by the General Land Office between 1862 and 1904, only 80 million acres went to homesteaders. Indeed, small farmers acquired more land under the Homestead Act in the 20th century than in the 19th.

Actual Homestead Act

CHAP. LXXV. —An Act to secure Homesteads to actual Settlers on the Public Domain.

Be it enacted by the Senate and House of Representatives of the United States of America in Congress assembled, That any person who is the head of a family, or who has arrived at the age of twenty-one years, and is a citizen of the United States, or who shall have filed his declaration of intention to become such, as required by the naturalization laws of the United States, and who has never borne arms against the United States Government or given aid and comfort to its enemies, shall, from and after the first January, eighteen hundred and sixty-three, be entitled to enter one quarter section or a less quantity of unappropriated public lands, upon which said person may have filed a preemption claim, or which may, at the time the application is made, be subject to preemption at one dollar and twenty-five cents, or less, per acre; or eighty acres or less of such unappropriated lands, at two dollars and fifty cents per acre, to be located in a body, in conformity to the legal subdivisions of the public lands, and after the same shall have been surveyed: Provided, That any person owning and residing on land may, under the provisions of this act, enter other land lying contiguous to his or her said land, which shall not, with the land so already owned and occupied, exceed in the aggregate one hundred and sixty acres.

SEC. 2. And be it further enacted, That the person applying for the benefit of this act shall, upon application to the register of the land office in which he or she is about to make such entry, make affidavit before the said register or receiver that he or she is the head of a family, or is twenty-one years or more of age, or shall have performed service in the army or navy of the United States, and that he has never borne arms against the Government of the United States or given aid and comfort to its enemies, and that such application is made for his or her exclusive use and benefit, and that said entry is made for the purpose of actual settlement and cultivation, and not either directly or indirectly for the use or benefit of any other person or persons whomsoever; and upon filing the said affidavit with the register or receiver, and on payment of ten dollars, he or she shall thereupon be permitted to enter the quantity of land specified: Provided, however, That no certificate shall be given or patent issued therefor until the expiration of five years from the date of such entry; and if, at the expiration of such time, or at any time within two years thereafter, the person making such entry; or, if he be dead, his widow; or in case of her death, his heirs or devisee; or in case of a widow making such entry, her heirs or devisee, in case of her death; shall. prove by two credible witnesses that he, she, or they have resided upon or cultivated the same for the term of five years immediately succeeding the time of filing the affidavit aforesaid, and shall make affidavit that no part of said land has been alienated, and that he has borne rue allegiance to the Government of the United States; then, in such case, he, she, or they, if at that time a citizen of the United States, shall be entitled to a patent, as in other cases provided for by law: And provided, further, That in case of the death of both father and mother, leaving an Infant child, or children, under twenty-one years of age, the right and fee shall ensure to the benefit of said infant child or children; and the executor, administrator, or guardian may, at any time within two years after the death of the surviving parent, and in accordance with the laws of the State in which such children for the time being have their domicile, sell said land for the benefit of said infants, but for no other purpose; and the purchaser shall acquire the absolute title by the purchase, and be entitled to a patent from the United States, on payment of the office fees and sum of money herein specified.

SEC. 3. And be it further enacted, That the register of the land office shall note all such applications on the tract books and plats of, his office, and keep a register of all such entries, and make return thereof to the General Land Office, together with the proof upon which they have been founded.

SEC. 4. And be it further enacted, That no lands acquired under the provisions of this act shall in any event become liable to the satisfaction of any debt or debts contracted prior to the issuing of the patent therefor.

SEC. 5. And be it further enacted, That if, at any time after the filing of the affidavit, as required in the second section of this act, and before the expiration of the five years aforesaid, it shall be proven, after due notice to the settler, to the satisfaction of the register of the land office, that the person having filed such affidavit shall have actually changed his or her residence, or abandoned the said land for more than six months at any time, then and in that event the land so entered shall revert to the government.

SEC. 6. And be it further enacted, That no individual shall be permitted to acquire title to more than one quarter section under the provisions of this act; and that the Commissioner of the General Land Office is hereby required to prepare and issue such rules and regulations, consistent with this act, as shall be necessary and proper to carry its provisions into effect; and that the registers and receivers of the several land offices shall be entitled to receive the same compensation for any lands entered under the provisions of this act that they are now entitled to receive when the same quantity of land is entered with money, one half to be paid by the person making the application at the time of so doing, and the other half on the issue of the certificate by the person to whom it may be issued; but this shall not be construed to enlarge the maximum of compensation now prescribed by law for any register or receiver: Provided, That nothing contained in this act shall be so construed as to impair or interfere in any manner whatever with existing preemption rights: And provided, further, That all persons who may have filed their applications for a preemption right prior to the passage of this act, shall be entitled to all privileges of this act: Provided, further, That no person who has served, or may hereafter serve, for a period of not less than fourteen days in the army or navy of the United States, either regular or volunteer, under the laws thereof, during the existence of an actual war, domestic or foreign, shall be deprived of the benefits of this act on account of not having attained the age of twenty-one years.

SEC. 7. And be it further enacted, That the fifth section of the act entitled "An act in addition to an act more effectually to provide for the punishment of certain crimes against the United States, and for other purposes," approved the third of March, in the year eighteen hundred and fifty-seven, shall extend to all oaths, affirmations, and affidavits, required or authorized by this act.

SEC. 8. And be it further enacted, That nothing in this act shall be so construed as to prevent any person who has availed him or herself of the benefits of the first section of this act, from paying the minimum price, or the price to which the same may have graduated, for the quantity of land so entered at any time before the expiration of the five years, and obtaining a patent therefor from the government, as in other cases provided by law, on making proof of settlement and cultivation as provided by existing laws granting preemption rights.

APPROVED, May 20, 1862.

Other Books by Gary W. Wietgrefe

- Lessons of an Immigrant Father, 1905 cattle drive 500 miles to Dakota
- Humor and Learning in a One-Room School
- Relating to Ancient Culture, and the mysterious agent changing it
- Relating to Ancient Learning, as it influences the 21st century
- Destination North Pole, 5000 km by bicycle
- Lakota Life After the Buffalo (by Victor Swallow)
- Women in the Life of Crazy Horse
- Living Beyond Fate (by Wesley N. Wietgrefe)
- Dakota Country Poems
- Life in Flight (Dakota poems)
- Proso Millet: A Farmer's Guide
- Proso Millet: A Trade Summary

www.ingramcontent.com/pod-product-compliance
Lightning Source LLC
Jackson TN
JSHW080740140526
102249JS00004B/11

* 9 7 9 8 9 9 4 1 9 6 8 3 0 *